THE NOAH PROJECT

The secrets of practical project management

◆

THE NOAH PROJECT

The secrets of practical project management

◆

Ralph L. Kliem
Irwin S. Ludin

Gower

Published by
Gower Publishing
Gower House
Croft Road
Aldershot
Hamphire GU11 3HR
England

Gower
Old Post Road
Brookfield
Vermont 05036
USA

Reprinted 1994

British Library Cataloguing in Publication Data

Kliem, Ralph L.
Project: Secrets of Practical Project Management
I. Title   II. Ludin, Irwin S.
658.404

ISBN 0–566–07439–7 Hardback
ISBN 0–566–07469–9 Paperback

Typeset in 10pt Garamond by Photoprint, Torquay, Devon
and printed in Great Britain by Hartnoll Ltd, Bodmin

Dawson
PO 409
£20·01

TO OUR BELOVED ANIMALS:

CHICA, RED DOG, AND MIDNIGHT – RLK

TOPO, DARLA, SWEETIE, PHOEBE, FARLEIGH, ABERDEEN,
DAISY, MINDY, MISTY, FOXY, OSWALD, ALBERT BOB,
AND QUEEN LATIFA – ISL

Contents

◆

Introduction

◆

Project management to many people is one of those fields with a body of knowledge that resides in the minds of only a few people. *The Noah Project* seeks to dispel that myth. Readers of all fields and industries can apply project management in a manner that can save them time and money, reduce their work effort, increase production, and make them more cost-effective.

The concepts, tools, and techniques described in this book work. The authors have used them effectively to manage projects, and so have thousands of other project managers in many different industries. You'll easily learn how to plan, organize, control, and lead a project from womb to tomb – efficiently, effectively, and effortlessly.

Although the characters and events are fictitious, the information imparted in each chapter is applicable to the real world. The scenes explain project management from the vantage point of David Michaels, a young executive for a private zoo. He must manage the dismantling of the zoo to a successful conclusion. He finds a mentor, Noah, who guides him through the project.

We chose the zoo to show that anyone in any environment can use project management. We also decided to use Noah as a mentor to show that anyone can use project management; to provide a unique perspective on project management; and to play with the reader's imagination. We chose the storyline of the Ark because almost everyone has heard of it and, if it did exist, took a miracle (perhaps project management?) to make it happen.

Here is just a sample of what you will learn from David Michael's experience and Noah's wisdom. For **planning**: drafting a statement of understanding; defining goals and objectives; creating meaningful estimates, work breakdown structures, and schedules; and identifying the critical path. For **organizing**: optimizing resource utilization; assigning roles and responsibilities; and preparing a project manual. For **controlling**: responding to changing requirements; collecting and assessing status; and conducting meetings efficiently and effectively. For **leading**: tackling morale problems; resolving morale problems; and encouraging teamwork.

So take a seat and turn the page to discover more about the hidden secrets of practical project management.

Ralph L. Kliem   Irwin S. Ludin

1

Proact, not react

◆

D avid Michaels sat behind his mahogany desk, elevated his feet upon it, and then placed his arms behind his head. A complete serenity overcame him and for a good reason. Everything at the zoo was running like a fine-tuned engine. No problems. None. He had everything under control as the manager of the Planning and Development Division of the zoo. At 26 years of age and two years out of school after receiving his MBA from an Ivy League college, his life could never have been better. Nothing, he felt, could stop him.

He heard the knob rattle on his office door. Suddenly the door flew open. In stepped a balding, overweight man in his mid-fifties. A cloud of brownish-grey smoke trailed behind him, originating from the thick cigar in his mouth.

"I've got some bad news," said Harrison Farnsworth, the executive director of the zoo and David's boss, as he leaned over David's desk.

"Bad news? What?" asked David. He dropped his feet back on the floor and sat upright in his chair.

"The Yuggenheim family is selling its ownership of the zoo," said Harrison. He went and pulled a chair up to the young executive's desk and sat in it.

"What does that have to do with anything? If the new owners won't keep us, we can always get a job at some other zoo," said David. "And the new keepers will take care of this place."

"Not so. Not so," said Harrison. He smashed his cigar into the ashtray on the desk. "The family sold the property to the Habeas Corporation. It's a major multinational firm which plans to transform the grounds into a large man-made landfill to dump industrial waste. The whole grounds could eventually become flooded with polluted waters."

"I don't believe it!"

"Doesn't matter if you do. The fact is that the Yuggenheim family wants the entire zoo dismantled and removed prior to delivery of the land to the company," said Harrison. A smile came to his face. "And they want us to conduct the project in exchange for employment with one of the firms that they currently own. They promise to double our salaries in our new positions." His smile faded. "But if we fail, no job, no future, no money!"

"And the animals? What will happen to them?" asked David. "I love those creatures. Who will take them? Where will they go? When must they move? The job is incredible. Is this possible?"

"That depends on how well you manage this project."

"How well I will manage this project?" he asked. He felt a chill crawl up his spine. "What is that supposed to mean?"

"It means that you are the project manager. I have to do other things prior to the day of the delivery of the zoo grounds to the company. The fate of this zoo is in your hands," said Harrison. He stood up from the chair. "You have ten months to the day to complete the project. The sooner you get started, the better for you and the animals. I've got other things to do. If you have any questions, feel free to see me. I will call by to see you from time to time. Goodbye and good luck." He turned and hurried out of the office.

David felt like a manic depressive, having gone from an extreme emotional high to an all-time low. How do I get started? What do I do first? I think I need a miracle, he thought. For the first time in his life he felt paralysed, unable to rise from his chair.

2

A project without goals and objectives is like a person without eyes or ears

◆

Resting his elbows on a chain-link fence, David started to feed the ducks floating on the pond. The thoughts floated in his mind as erratically as the ducks on the water.

"I can't believe this is happening. There are over 3000 animals in the zoo. We've got everything from cockatoos to kangaroos, from rabbits to piranhas. What the hell am I going to do? I don't have the faintest idea as to where to start. My mind is flooded with details," David mumbled.

"Did you say flood, young man?" asked an old man. His navy blue Greek fisherman's cap covered his silver grey hair that touched below his neckline. His beard matched his hair in both colour and length. A porcelain pipe hung from his mouth emitting a stream of smooth flowing, cherry smelling smoke. Brown leather deck shoes graced his feet.

"Pardon me, mister?" David stepped back, thinking that the old man was another street bum asking for money. He wondered even in the first place how the old geezer got in the zoo.

"Flood. Did I hear you say the word 'flood?'" asked the old man. He moved closer to David.

"Yeah. What's it to you?" What a nosy old man, thought David.

"I know all about floods. And I don't mean the toilet tank overflow type, either," said the old man. "Why, I commanded one of the greatest sailing vessels of all time. And it was during a flood. Way back in '48."

"There was no great flood in '48," said David. What a strange fellow, he thought. He turned and started to walk away.

"Wait. Yes there was, in '48. That's 2448 BC! And it was the big one. It rained for 40 days and 40 nights. The waters started receding 150 days later. I'm Noah. Maybe you've heard of me?"

"Noah? You've got to be kidding!" David stopped and turned to face the old man. "The same old fogey they talk about in the Bible who filled his boat with animals to protect them from the great flood? I don't believe you."

"Yes I am, the very same. Most people have heard of me. And my story."

"If you are Noah, then give me a simple solution to my problem."

"A solution I can provide; but a simple one I'm not so sure about," said Noah. "A simple solution, you see, takes a combination of experience, knowledge, skill, timing, and luck. These factors combined with four special secrets will enable you to succeed. That's how I built the Ark. And you probably remember that the Ark was big. But do you know how big?"

"Big enough to hold you and your family, all the animals, food for the trip, and a refuse holding area. So I'd guess about a football stadium's worth in size."

"Good guess, sonny. You're close. The Ark measured 450 feet long by 75 feet wide by 45 feet high. And that translates roughly into 570 of today's railroad cars of cabin space. And it weighed about 25 million pounds unloaded. It was one fine craft," said Noah. A proud smile showed through the blanket of beard.

"OK, enough of the reminiscing. What are these secrets? I don't have all day to listen to some old man claiming to be Noah," said David.

"You're a testy young chap. And in quite a rush, too. Must be pretty important stuff you're working on. I like you, but your style could use some refining. Tell you what I'm going to do. I'll help you," said Noah.

"Sure, sure. Go on. I need all the help I can get."

"Now that you're aware of the magnitude of my effort, hazard a guess as to how long it took to build the Ark. And I'll give you a hint. I had a staff of three men full-time," said Noah.

"Let's see . . . hmmm . . . three men full-time for 12 months less vacation, holidays, and sick-leave times the productivity factor yields . . . I'd estimate ten years," guessed David.

"You're not even close. One hundred and twenty years to the day I started. Like I said, it was one fine craft." Noah looked toward the sky as if receiving a calling from God. Then he stared into the young man's eyes.

"All right, so you've got a reputation. I accept your offer to help me," said David. "What have I got to lose? So what's the first secret?"

"You indirectly know the first secret. You referred to it in a roundabout way several times already. You just haven't recognized it as a secret yet. Tell me, what exactly is your job? What are you supposed to achieve?" asked Noah. He led David over to a bench facing the ducks and sat down.

"What do you mean, what am I supposed to achieve? Obviously I have to completely remove all the animals and dismantle the entire zoo facility before the delivery of the grounds to the Habeas Corporation. It's that simple."

"You think that's it, huh? Do you have it in writing?"

"What are you talking about?" asked David. "No, it's not written down anywhere. My boss told me about it this morning."

"Have you ever taken any legal classes? Ever watch any detective or private eye shows on TV? One of the first questions asked is 'Do you have any documentation?'. A straightforward, easy to read document stating the goals, objectives, and deliverables of your project defines your charter," said Noah.

"That's a good point, Noah. A simple document, you say, telling the overall goals and objectives of the project with the major deliverables. And maybe even include the essential tasks to build them."

"Now you're thinking. And you might want to put in a section on responsible parties."

"Yeah, that makes sense. Good sense," said David. "But what do I do with it? What purpose does it serve?"

"This document answers the question 'Who does what for whom and why'. And it's in black and white. You now have something concrete to work with instead of hot air. This will help your team as well as your client keep on track to build the right job and get it done. It's called a statement of understanding."

"So, it helps build more effective communications among team members and the client. But who is my client?" asked David.

"Who do you think?"

"My boss?"

Noah raised his index finger to make a point. "That's correct."

"Then by documenting the project in the form of a statement of understanding, he can't come back to me and say that he told me something which maybe he didn't. That does make sense. It also pinpoints what I have to do exactly," said David. "But when you built the Ark, did you develop one?"

"Not only does it pinpoint what you have to do, it also specifies what everybody else has to do. And yes, I had one also. It only makes sense. And eliminates confusion and duplication of effort."

"OK, I see the purpose of the statement of understanding. Great. But do you have a copy of the one you developed when building the Ark? I'd like to see it so I have a good idea of what one looks like," said David. He knew that this was the test to find out if the old man was a charlatan.

"Sure, sonny. I have it, but you can't have it."

I knew he was a fraud, thought David. "Well, where is it? If you have it, I'd like you to flaunt it. Or at least let me take a peek at it."

Noah shook his head back and forth and started to rise.

"You think I carry it in my pocket or what? Look, do you have a pencil and some paper?" asked Noah.

David pulled some paper and a pencil out of his shirt pocket. "Here you go," said David. He sat back on the bench.

"Thanks. I'll sketch it out for you." Noah gave a grateful smile.

STATEMENT OF UNDERSTANDING

Purpose:	To provide direction to prepare the Ark.
Scope:	Identifies constraints to consider before and during the Ark preparation.
Objectives:	To define necessary elements to meet with the Ark's requirements.
Background:	States a brief overview of Ark work involved including past, present, and future.

References:	Reflects previous Ark studies carried out.
Organizational Chart:	Defines Ark hierarchy roles and responsibilities.
Considerations and Assumptions:	Establishes high-level tasks to perform and determines the meeting of those tasks; specifies special factors and activities; and identifies interface relationships.

"But that can't be all to getting a project off to a good start. The statement of understanding must lead to something." David's fears that the old man was a phoney had disappeared.

"Yes, it does," said Noah. "It leads to the work breakdown structure."

"A work breakdown structure? What is that?" David suddenly realized he was no longer talking to an old fool.

"It's a top-down listing of all tasks and subtasks required to complete the project. Then you develop a schedule based upon the work breakdown structure and some time estimates. But all that leads to something more important. The first secret."

"I don't understand. What is it?" asked David.

"I don't know why I am doing this. You're just some punk kid." said Noah. He started to rise from the bench.

"Wait. I'm no punk. I graduated with distinction from an Ivy League college, and have five years' experience in my field," said David.

"Is that so? You have five years one time or one year five times?" Noah sat back down on the bench.

"Huh?"

Noah's voice softened. "Anyway, you remind me of one of my sons. And I guess that's why I want to help you."

"But Noah, you still haven't told me the first secret."

"I think you already know it, but haven't realized it as yet. All this time we've been talking about . . ."

"Planning!" said David. "It's planning. That's the first secret. I should have known. Of course, it's all so simple now. Why didn't I think of it? I should plan before doing anything. But you taught me more than just planning, Noah."

"Oh?"

"Patience," said David. "You taught me patience. I wanted to jump into the project right away, but I lacked the patience. You kept telling me to slow down, indirectly. Brilliant, Noah. Now I can make things happen."

"See you later, same time same place in two days. Look at it as a status meeting. 'Bye." Noah rose from the bench and disappeared in the large crowd passing by.

"Noah? Noah? Where are you, Noah?" David shouted as he, too, jumped from the bench and joined the crowd. But Noah was nowhere. How did you disappear so fast like that? he thought. I need you!

3

The priority often depends on who's in authority

◆

David eased the door open to Harrison's office. He stuck his head through the narrow opening and confronted a cloud of thick cigar smoke. "Have you got a minute?"

"Yeah," said Farnsworth. He placed his pen on the mahogany desk and sat back in his leather-bound chair. "What?"

"I had the opportunity to take some time to solidify in my mind just exactly what you want to achieve with the project," said David. He sat down in a chair facing the boss's desk. "And I wrote it down. Do you have a few minutes to read it? It's only two pages." He laid the document on the desk.

Harrison picked it up. "Sure. Let's see . . . Right. The project must end by that date. The project must achieve those goals and deliverables within the allocated budget . . . Yeah. The major tasks are correct and the support required to perform those tasks is not unrealistic. What gave you the idea to write this up? It's great. What? Wait a minute . . . You want me to sign this?"

"That's the best part. By both of us signing it, it shows that we agree on what needs to be achieved and under what conditions," said David. "You know, it means we start off on the same wavelength, so to speak."

"I see. It's a communication tool. All right, I'll sign it. A little formal for just the two of us, but at least it will prevent anything from falling through the cracks." Harrison scribbled his signature on the bottom of the form and tossed the document over to David.

"That's right, and it gets me off to the right start. There's just one more thing," said David as he picked up the document, folded it, and stashed it in his shirt pocket.

"What's that?"

"I need to do something else."

"Like what?" asked Harrison.

"Like develop a work breakdown structure."

"A what?"

David's throat became dry for fear of not explaining it right. "A work breakdown structure is a listing of the tasks required to achieve the goals identified in the statement of understanding."

"Oh, I see. What does that involve?"

"The traditional two. Time and resources," said David.

"I don't know," snapped Harrison. "You don't have much of either. Can you be more specific?"

"I need to get input from those people who know something about related topics concerning the project."

"You need to talk to a few people, right?"

"Right," said David.

Harrison scribbled on a notepad some names and numbers of people, and ripped off the sheet and handed it to David. "It's a list of people you can talk to. They should all cooperate. Tell them I sent you and that they are assigned to the initial project team. At the very least, you'll get your listing of tasks for the work breakdown structure."

"Great."

"Is there anything else?" asked Harrison.

"Yes. There's just one more thing," said David. He sensed that Harrison was anxious for him to leave.

"You said that before. Is this it?"

"Yes."

"I don't want you to spend too much time planning and too little time doing," warned Harrison.

"So that I don't have enough time to complete the project?" asked David. He waited for a response. Then it came.

"No, of course not," said Harrison. "I meant . . . "

"By planning properly, I'll save time. It requires a little patience but . . ."

"Look, you have only a short time to complete this project. I don't want you to yield to analysis paralysis. What else do you need to do, just out of curiosity?" Harrison lit a new cigar and puffed vigorously on it.

"I need to do other planning." David waved his right arm back and forth to keep the smoke from clouding his vision. "It's important to see where we're going on this project."

"OK, the statement of understanding is fine. So is putting together the work breakdown structure. But any other stuff, I don't know. I'm not convinced that it will help. Like I said, it seems to take too much time and effort. I'll give you a chance, though. Build a case. And keep it short. There's not enough time to practise this stuff you learned in college. This is the real world. Now it's time to get back to work."

"I'm on my way," said David. He gave Harrison a smile. Now I'll show him how to really manage a project, he thought as he left the office. This old buzzard will be taking lessons from me!

4

Build your project's work breakdown structure

◆

As he walked along the fence that corralled the llamas, tapirs, and ponies, David's mind raced a mile a minute.

It just makes good common sense, thought David. I don't understand it. Taking time to plan leads to more time to complete the project. You know where you're going. I just don't understand how . . . He felt a tap on his shoulder and turned around.

"Hey there sonny, what are you doing? Sitting down on the job?" asked Noah.

"Whhhat? Oh, it's you." David noticed that Noah was still wearing his fisherman's cap and deck shoes and holding his porcelain pipe.

"Who'd you think it was? The Hulk?" asked Noah with a sarcastic grin. "How's your project going? I bet you're moving it right along."

"Sorry. It's not what you think. It's just that I tried to implement what you taught me earlier. Quite frankly, it's easier said than done," said David.

"Yes, many things are easier said than done. But where's your sense of challenge?"

"Let's walk around while we talk. You're right again, Noah. My boss says it takes too much time and effort to plan anything. And, after a short discussion with him, I think he's right."

"Really, now?"

"Look, Noah, I see the validity of what you say. It makes good sense. But . . ."

"But what? Did he understand the concept and beauty of a statement of understanding?"

"Yes, he liked the statement of understanding. He thought it was great. He even liked the idea of putting together a work breakdown structure. And he gave me some names of people to see for input," said David.

"Speaking of input, I have an idea," said Noah.

"Yeah? What is it? I'm all ears." David stopped walking.

"I'm glad that you're listening," said Noah as he came to a halt. "You know that God gave us two ears and one mouth so that we can listen twice as much as we speak. But seriously, why don't you put together a straw horse . . ."

"Excuse me for interrupting, but what does arts and crafts have to do with my project?"

"Nothing. A straw horse is a first cut at defining your product; in your case the work breakdown structure," said Noah. He started walking again.

"Drafting a work breakdown structure?" asked David. He followed Noah. "That's a good idea. Look, I understand the concept of a work breakdown structure. But what does one look like?"

"I knew you'd ask," said Noah. "So I'll show you a sample of what mine looked like." He yanked a piece of paper and a pencil from his shirt pocket, leaned against the wall of a hut, and drafted a work breakdown structure. He handed the paper to David.

WORK BREAKDOWN STRUCTURE

1.0   Ark definition
1.1   Identify requirements
1.2   Draft plan

2.0   Ark design
2.1   Prepare specifications
2.2   Establish design

3.0   Ark construction
3.1   Loft parts
    3.1.1   Fashion keel
    3.1.2   Lift keel onto blocks
    3.1.3   Bolt floors to keel
    3.1.4   Attach stem to keel
    3.1.5   Attach sternpost to keel
    3.1.6   Attach keelson to floor
3.2   Fashion ark

4.0   Ark implementation
4.1   Obtain supplies
4.2   Gather animals

5.0   Ark refinements
5.1   Make modifications

"Each section represents a product or subproduct which, in turn, is exploded into tasks and, if need be, into subtasks," continued Noah. "You'll notice that the description for a product and subproducts includes an adjective and noun and each task and subtask has an active verb and object. Also, note that a series of numbers are shown in each section to reflect the level of the product, subproduct, task, or subtask within the work breakdown structure."

"After I draft the work breakdown structure, I can then review it with the people on the list. That's great," said David. Excitement overcame him. If anything, he thought, I could use the work breakdown structure as a checklist. He followed Noah as they moved through the crowd.

Noah pointed his finger at David. "Don't forget the signatures."

"What do the signatures gain me?"

"Just as the signatures on the statement of understanding ensure commitment, so do the signatures on the work breakdown structure. And when people have an opportunity to draw up their work they also generate a desire not only to perform, but also to go the extra mile," said Noah.

"Makes sense. Once I have their input, I can then go to the boss and say 'Look, we've expended this much time and effort in building the work breakdown structure, now let's realize its benefits'. Besides, what good is a work breakdown structure all by itself?" asked David.

"Not so fast. A work breakdown structure without signatures does have merit," said Noah. "It identifies the task listing. The signatures, however, offer commitment and validate the information contained within."

"He can't help but see the value of such detail," said David.

"He's a big picture man. Don't bother him with details."

"But I can still hear him making the same old arguments, Noah."

"What's his biggest gripe?"

"Lack of time."

"Tell him that planning saves time in the long run."

"I told him that."

"So?"

"He understood," said David. "It's just that he wants to see action right away."

"Aesop's contradictions apply here. Aesop said that he who hesitates is lost. Aesop also said that haste makes waste. The thing is, each statement is correct. The trick is to know when each applies," said Noah, puffing on his pipe.

"I can hear it now," said David. He raised his hands in a expression of helplessness. "Lack of planning skills exists. Ditto for lack of budget. He'll also say that too much time will be spent in trying to getting everyone to cooperate."

Noah removed his pipe and pointed the mouthpiece at David. "It boils down to togetherness. You, your boss, your team. You're all in it together. And together you'll either sink or swim. So focus on functioning like a team. Your boss will appreciate that."

"He certainly wants everyone to cooperate," said David. "But he'll just say that it's more important to get the job done than getting everyone to like each other."

"It's not the same thing. All this planning will get people to cooperate with one another. It builds consensus which improves communication, which improves morale and generates enthusiasm," said Noah as he put the pipe back in his mouth.

"Cooperation is what it's all about. At least that's what I thought."

"We're doing a lot of talking here. It's about time for action. Meet with the people your boss recommended. One-to-one at first. Tell them that there will be a group discussion after you compile the results of the one-to-one. And that you'll send them a memo identifying date, time, and place. The sooner you do it, the sooner you can start on the work breakdown structure," said Noah.

David nodded his head. "That's a good idea. It's better to start this endeavour earlier in a project than later on. Once I complete the work breakdown structure and get everyone's approval — and that includes obtaining their signatures — I'll show my boss."

"And what do you think he'll say?"

"He can't help but encourage me to build a schedule and acquire estimates. It just makes good sense. You know, it really is a matter of having the desire to do these things. There's really no other explanation," said David.

"There is an explanation. Desire comes with maturity. And eventually this desire evolves into routine nature."

"I still have another question, Noah." David talked as he stared at the lions pacing to and fro.

"Go ahead."

"How will I handle," asked David, "building the schedule and calculating estimates?"

"The same way as you will build your work breakdown structure. Look, once you build your work breakdown structure I'll let you in on the next secret. Same place, same time, in two days," said Noah.

David turned his attention to Noah. "Noah, you never . . . Noah . . . Where are you? How does that guy disappear so fast?" mumbled David. He looked about and noticed that the old man had manoeuvred himself close to the main exit of the zoo. He then slipped away with a departing crowd. You're a shrewd one, he thought. No doubt about that. I hope I can manoeuvre as easily as you.

5

You can't have precise estimates

◆

He sat behind his desk developing planning. Piles of paper lay scattered across David's desk as his hands worked furiously on one pile.

Let's see . . . That's it. This drafted plan is just the thing I need. If I just explode the work breakdown structure a little more, I'll have a detailed listing of the tasks, thought David. There, that's not bad for a draft. I'll be able to flesh it out more when I review it with the folks that the old man recommended.

He heard pounding on his office door.

"What? Who's there? Come in." He looked up and saw an unexpected visitor standing at the entrance.

"I stopped by to see how things are going," said Harrison. A plume of smoke encircled his head. He grabbed a chair and sat next to David.

"Everything's moving along. Quite well. I'm putting together a draft of the work breakdown structure that we talked about earlier," said David.

"I still don't quite understand how that will help anything," said Harrison.

"Have you got a minute?" asked David. He felt confident about what he produced. "I think you'll see its value after I show you what I've put together."

Harrison looked at his watch as he puffed on his cigar, creating a volcanic plume. "Sure, but don't spend too much time on this effort. We've got work to do."

"As you can see here, I've written on the top of the page 'Zoo dismantlement' which is the result of this project," said David. His finger pointed to the top of the work breakdown structure and moved towards the bottom of the page. "I then broke down the relocation into deliverables, or major components. I have three. Here's a list of all the tasks needed to build each deliverable. In some cases, I exploded some tasks into subtasks in order to get a more definitive listing of what needs to be accomplished."

"I see. But how far down do you explode a work breakdown structure?" asked Harrison.

"Several rules of thumb exist," explained Michaels. "The most common is to do so until a task cannot be subdivided further. Another is that when you eventually estimate how long each task takes, and if that estimate exceeds 80 hours, you explode the task into subtasks."

"Those sound like good rules of thumb. OK, so you have the work breakdown structure. What now?"

"I will go to the people you recommended," said David. "They appear to be experts in producing each of the deliverables and I'll talk with them and get their input. I'll also work on getting their commitment. Signatures of commitment. If I can't, I'll revise the draft until it meets with their approval. Then they'll be more inclined to sign it."

"That makes sense, and it encourages team building. OK, then what?"

"According to Noah . . . " David caught his slip of the tongue.

"What? Noah? Who are you talking about?"

"Sorry, never mind. I was thinking of something else. Anyway, I'll make another pass and talk with these people to get their opinions and feedback on how long it takes to perform each task," said David.

"On everything listed on the work breakdown structure? That would take forever, and we don't have that much time . . . "

"No, not on everything," said David. He smiled to himself because he had anticipated Harrison's objections and was prepared for them. "Just on those tasks and subtasks that cannot be exploded further."

"I see. But how do you estimate them?"

"The best approach is to use the three-point formula according to what I read just a little while ago. For each task or subtask you determine how much time it takes to perform under a pessimistic or worst-case scenario; the optimistic or best-case scenario; and the most likely time you'd usually expect the task will take to complete. After multiplying the most likely time estimate by four, add that figure to the most pessimistic and most optimistic ones and divide this sum total by six. This result is how you derive your estimate of how long it takes to complete a task," said David. "Here's what the formula looks like." He scribbled the formula on a piece of paper.

$$\frac{\text{Most pessimistic} + (4 \times \text{Most likely}) + \text{Most optimistic}}{6}$$

He handed the paper to Harrison.

"Here's an example to move the elephants from the zoo," continued David. He scribbled on another piece of paper as Harrison looked on. "Our most optimistic estimate is 30 hours; most likely is 40; and most pessimistic is 80. So [30 + (4 × 40) + 80] ÷ 6 equals [30 + 160 + 80] ÷ 6 equals 45. And that's the estimate we'll use."

"So, you do that for each task in the work breakdown structure that can't be exploded down further," said Harrison.

"That's right."

"But for your work breakdown structure that looks like it will take quite a long time. And we don't have . . . "

"Excuse me, boss," interrupted David. He had waited for this moment. "If you want good plans, you have to work smart at getting good estimates. A friend of mine says that an estimate is only a predictor of the future. The more information you have to predict with, the higher the reliability of your prediction. And with it come more useful plans and eventual execution of those plans. Also, in this century of computers, I'm going to build it using a spreadsheet software package to perform all the calculations so it won't take as long as you think."

"Makes sense. Sounds like your friend is pretty wise."

"You could say that."

"All right. Say the estimates are complete. What's next?"

"A network diagram," said David. Go ahead, he thought. Ask me any question. I'm ready for you. Shoot. I've read all about these diagrams.

"A what?"

"A network diagram. It's a scheduling tool."

"So how do you build one of these network diagrams?" asked Harrison. "What's the purpose of yet another tool? I said that I only had a few minutes to talk with you, but you've caught my attention."

"Ahhhh . . . Ahmmmm," said David.

How do you build a network diagram? thought David. The palms of his hands became moist and his throat dry.

The phone rang. David grabbed the receiver on the first ring. It was not for him.

"It's for me? How did Miss Wright know I was here with you? She's a fine secretary," said Harrison. He grabbed the receiver from David.

"Right . . . Yes . . . right . . . I see," said Harrison. He then hung up the receiver. "David, something urgent I need to attend to. I'll be back. I like what you're doing. Keep it up." He rushed out of the office.

David looked out from his office window and up into the grey clouds hovering above the zoo. "Thank you, God," he said softly. "Thank you."

6

A network diagram is your road map

◆

Ambling about in the primate house with his hands buried in his pockets David watched the chimpanzees who were surrounded by wooden blocks of various colours and sizes. They looked as if their efforts only seemed to result in confusion. His mind then turned to other matters.

Schedules, schedules, schedules, he thought. How do you construct schedules? I know it has something to do with the work breakdown structure. And the network diagram must show more than just interdependencies between activities. But how do I make the transformation?

"Hey there. You look kind of worried. Problems?"

David turned in the direction of the voice. He noticed right away the hat and the shoes and the pipe. "Noah! I've got to talk with you. I know we were to meet tomorrow but to tell you the truth I need to talk with you now. Can you spare a few minutes?"

"What seems to concern you? Is it your work breakdown structure?"

"No, my boss loved the work breakdown structure idea. You were right. I showed him my draft and right away he saw the significance of what I'm doing. He's even interested in what comes after the work breakdown structure, estimating." David led Noah to a bench against the wall and sat down.

"Did you elaborate on any techniques?" asked Noah. He sat next to David.

"I did," said David. "He liked the three-point estimating technique I read about. He said, though, that it takes a long time to do it. I told him I would run it on my computer."

"That's good. It's better to work smart, not hard."

"Noah, he bought it all — hook, line, and sinker."

"So?"

"So he asked a question I couldn't answer." David rubbed his fingers through his hair.

"What did you do?"

"I didn't have to do anything. He received an urgent phone call and had to leave. I guess you could say that this was a case where I was saved by the bell," said David with a grin.

"You need some help."

"Cute, real cute Noah. I guess you're right. I do need you. It's just with my MBA and all, I felt confident. I was wrong. I need some guidance."

"You know what confidence is?" asked Noah. "It's the feeling you have before you know better. So, you'd like me to get involved? Well, I had some expert help when I built the Ark. We all need a helping hand in this world." He looked up at the ceiling of the primate house and then at David.

"You were luckier than most, Noah. You had in your corner not only the powers to be but the power that is. And that's strong stuff."

Noah chuckled. "OK, let her rip, sonny."

"How do you construct a network diagram?" asked David. "What does it look like?"

"You've already compiled a comprehensive list of all the tasks and subtasks which your project comprises. Now you have to put these pieces of the puzzle together in a meaningful way," said Noah.

"I think I get it now. I need to sequence logically the tasks and subtasks together," said David. "Mentally, I can see how they relate, but visually how do you show it?"

"I see I'm going to have to lead you by the hand." Noah rose from the bench and picked up a flattened empty box of popcorn. He returned to the bench and sketched a diagram. He laid the box on David's lap but kept a finger on its surface. "OK, here's a sampling of what mine looked like:"

Noah's finger pounded on the box as he talked. "Each rectangle represents a task or subtask in the work breakdown structure that cannot be exploded into further detail. The tasks or subtasks are called activities. The arrows between rectangles show dependencies between activities and the logic of the schedules."

"OK. Having shown the sequence of activities, now what?" asked David. "The flow is defined here. Right?"

"Right, Noah."

"Now that I know how I am to proceed, I can estimate how long it takes to perform these tasks."

"The estimates?" asked David. "Of course I remember them. A piece of cake."

"Estimate using hours, maybe. Then you can convert those hours into days, weeks, whatever."

"That makes sense. I take the estimate for each task, and convert the hours into days. Then, I can identify the start and stop dates for each activity." David felt that he knew everything about scheduling. "Well, that should do it."

"Not yet," said Noah. "You might want to be aware that there are really four dates associated with each activity." Noah grabbed the box and started writing as he talked. "Now here's how to calculate these dates using the formulas. I'll use the network diagram I just drew for you. I'll mark the

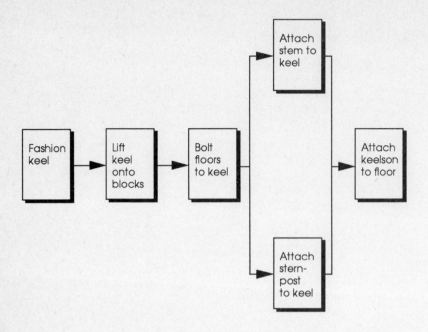

Figure 6.1 Network diagram for keel

duration for each activity and assign, for simplicity, an activity number for each one. Then I'll explain everything."

Noah added the durations and the activity numbers to the rectangles along with the results of some quick calculations.

"Now to calculate the dates for each task, you need to move through the network diagram from left to right. This is called the forward pass. You do this to calculate the early start and finish dates.

"You see that activity number one takes two days to complete. That means it starts on day one and finishes at close of business on day two. Knowing that the activity begins on day one, you add the duration of two days to day one which totals three days. That doesn't make sense because it should end on day two. That's why you subtract one, so the activity is scheduled to end on the right day. With me so far?"

"You bet," said David. His head started to ache from the deep concentration.

"Good. It's important that you understand the concept. Now, keeping in mind the logic of the network diagram, let's assume that activity number two begins right after activity number one finishes. That is, number two begins on day three. It has a duration of two days, meaning it completes on day . . ."

"Five," said David.

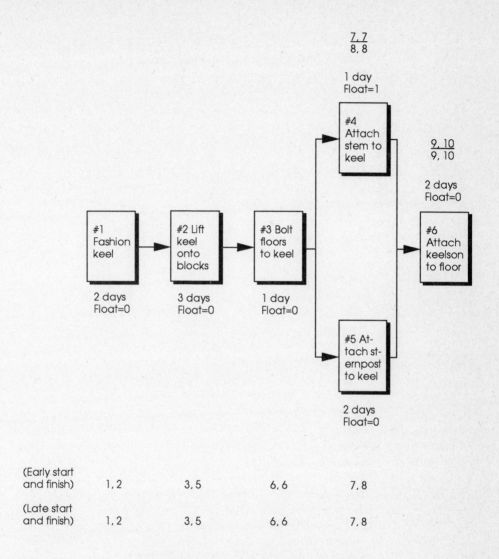

Figure 6.2 Network diagram for keel

"That's it." Noah then scribbled on top of the box. "I'll finish the rest of the calculations. It all follows the same idea. There, now that we have the early start and finish dates for each activity we can calculate the late start and finish dates. Ready?"

"You bet," said David. His concentration paid off. He understood completely.

"This time we do something different. We'll move through the network diagram from right to left. That's called a backward pass. We know that activity number six, therefore, must have a late start date of nine because you subtract the duration of two days from day ten which equals eight. Then you add one, which gives you a late start of nine. Keeping in mind the logic of the schedule you look at the activity for the preceding activity, which is number four and number five. Let's look at number five.

"You know that number five finishes before number six can begin. That means number five must have a late finish of eight. Since number five has a duration of two days, it must have a late start of seven, if you keep in mind the formula for calculating the late start of any activity. You repeat this step for activity number four. With me?"

David nodded his head.

"Good. Now you know that both activities number four and number five run parallel but have different durations," continued Noah. "You consider the late start of the activity with the longest duration and use its late start date to determine the late finish date for the preceding activity, which is activity number three. You repeat these steps until you've calculated the late start and finish dates for all activities." Noah did just that and recorded the results in the network diagram.

"We're ready to determine the critical path. It's simple. Notice that some activities have the same early and late dates?"

"Yeah," said David. He pointed to activity numbers one, two, three, five and six.

"You've got it. That's the critical path. You'll note that these activities have a float of zero. By subtracting the early start from the late start," continued Noah, "except one. That's activity number four. It has a late start of eight and an early start of seven. That gives a float of one day," said Noah.

"Four dates? How come so many?"

"Well, there's the early start, early finish, late start, and late finish dates."

"That does add up to four dates. What's the purpose? Isn't it a bit confusing?" asked David.

"Not really. The early start date identifies the earliest date, or time, that an event can start. The early finish date identifies the earliest date, or time an event can finish. The late start date identifies the latest date, or time an event can start . . ." said Noah.

"And I bet the late finish identifies the latest time an event can finish," said David. He couldn't wait to get started. He rose from the bench.

"That's right. And sit down, sonny. You're not through," continued Noah. "For my Ark project I also calculated — excuse the expression, float time. Float time is also called slack time. This is the time period between the latest date an activity can take place without extending the project's delivery date and the earliest date an activity can be expected to take place."

David sat back on the bench. "So those dates not only tell when events can start and finish but also enable me to calculate how much time I can let a task slip without affecting my project's completion date. Great, it's all coming together. Noah, you're a Godsend."

Noah grabbed the popcorn box from David and scribbled some mathematical expressions. He then gave back the box to David and pointed at it. "Let me show you something. Here are the formulas I used for calculating the dates and helping me to identify the critical path for my project:"

$$\text{Early start} = \text{Early finish} - \text{Duration} + 1$$
$$\text{Early finish} = \text{Early start} + \text{Duration} - 1$$
$$\text{Late start} = \text{Late finish} - \text{Duration} + 1$$
$$\text{Late finish} = \text{Late start} + \text{Duration} - 1$$

"These formulas also tell me my critical path? Wow! That's great! By the way, what's a critical path?" asked David.

"See the network I drew?" He moved his crooked finger through the network diagram on the box. "On it is one unique path that is the longest. There is no path longer than this one over the duration of my project. Other paths are either equal to or less than its time span. And, the early and late start and finish dates match up."

"So what?"

"Sew it yourself, David. Look, what do you think I am? A tailor? By knowing the critical path you help ensure the successful delivery of your project. It provides two major fundamental pieces of information. The critical path has no float or slack time. So any schedule slippage on this path will, in fact, cause a slippage of the project's delivery date. That is, unless the event's slippage can be recovered somehow downstream. No pun intended," continued Noah. "And you have a clear understanding of the events that are critical to the successful delivery of your project. So, you can take a close look and keep tabs on what's happening to them. It also value-adds to the project's performance as a whole. With these two pieces of information, you can do 'what-if's' for resource allocation. You can take advantage of slack periods to re-allocate your resources and still guarantee successful project delivery. That's how it helped me."

"You sure have a lot of breath in you to talk for so long without stopping." David grew impatient with the lecture. His gaze turned from Noah to the chimpanzees.

"OK, so enough for the lecture. And look at me, sonny. It's for your own good. Do you understand what I'm getting at?"

David gave Noah his fullest attention. "Sure," he said confidently. "The activities that have zero float are the ones I can't let slide or else I won't meet my project's completion date. So to reiterate, the critical path has three characteristics: first, the tasks on it have zero float; second, the early and late start and finish dates match; and third, the tasks on it are on the longest path of the network diagram."

Noah then spoke. "You also have to remember that the world is a changing place. And as circumstances change, so does the critical path. Just be sure to know when to make the change. And to understand current implications and nuances."

"It sounds so simple, and it makes good common sense. But how do I get consensus for the schedule dates? The same way that I get the work breakdown structure and estimates?" asked David.

"Yes." Noah rose from the bench.

"I still have to do that, you know, get feedback and consensus on the work breakdown structure," said David as he looked up at Noah. "Then I have to calculate the estimates. And then generate the schedules. Oh well, that shouldn't prove too much of a problem. Tomorrow I meet with the first person on the list. You mentioned 'what-ifs' earlier. So what if I should have problems? How can I get in contact with you?"

"Call me. I have a Freephone number. It's Freephone–NOAH."

"Let me write that down," said David. He removed his billfold and wrote the number on a business card. "How did you get a Freephone number?" He looked up and noticed the old man was gone. "Noah, where are you? Noah?" He did it again, thought David, as he scratched his head.

7

Feedback is not automatic; you must seek it

◆

David had his feet propped up on his desk while he scribbled on a notepad resting on his lap. His temples pounded from the deep thought that tore at his mind. His concentration broke upon hearing a knock on the door. "Come in," he said, sitting upright in his chair. He watched the door swing open.

"Ted! Let's go over to the round table in the corner. I'd like to get your opinion on something," said David.

He could always pick Ted from a crowd. The man had long black sideburns and short curly hair that was heavily streaked with grey. His face was always a bright red which led David to sometimes mistakenly believe the man was angry. David jumped to his feet and proffered his hand as he approached Ted.

"Sure thing," said Ted without a smile. "What do you have?" He did not bother to shake David's hand but sat at the table.

David made a point of sitting next to Ted rather than on the other side of the table. "We're all aware of the zoo's disposition based on the new ownership. My job is to make the transition happen."

"I know that, Michaels. So what do you want from me?" Ted folded his arms across his chest.

David pointed to a large sheet of paper blanketing the table. "I'm putting together a plan to manage this project. What I'd like is your opinion on this. It's a work breakdown structure for conducting the zoo transition."

"I see . . . Look, right from the start I'm not thrilled about this. I've been here a long time and have done a good job. So they sell the zoo grounds and I'm out of a job. I didn't even mess up or anything. It's not my fault. I have a family to feed and care for. The whole thing stinks," said Ted.

"I understand your feelings, Ted. Nevertheless we have a job to do in the remaining ten months," said David. He noticed that Ted tightened his grip on his forearms and his voice became harsh. "Who knows, we may all still be employed if this works."

"Yeah, yeah," said Ted. "I've heard the story before. Work hard. Do a good job. The company will take care of you. They're going to take care of me all right. All of us. I can hardly wait."

"Ted, you're the head man for the Maintenance and Horticulture Division of our zoo. You have a lot of responsibilities." David noticed that Ted started to uncross his arms. "And you do commendable work. If we all pull together, there's a good chance that we'll have a golden opportunity. Otherwise . . ."

"Sure, sure," said Ted. "So, tell me what you've got here."

"What I have done is to identify those tasks and subtasks which are required to complete our project."

"Hmm. I see. What's this listing called?"

"A work breakdown structure," said David. He watched as Ted leaned forward in his chair.

"Interesting, Michaels."

"The work breakdown structure identifies the effort for the entire project. Let me explain what pertains to you."

David spent the next 30 minutes reviewing and revising the work breakdown structure with Ted.

"Well, what do you think?" asked David.

"I think if you add those few tasks and subtasks to the work breakdown structure that I mentioned and explode these others down into more refined detail, you will find it more representative of what needs to be done. Anyway, that's my perspective," said Ted. This time he cracked a smile.

"Good. The breakdown does look better already."

"Glad to be of help, David. Anything else? Or am I free to go?"

David noticed that Ted called him by his first name. "Ah, would you mind initialling here?" He pointed to a blank portion on the page. "It just means that I reviewed the work breakdown structure with you and that you concur with your portions."

"Well, I don't know . . ." Ted crossed his arms.

"What's the matter?"

"It's just that you didn't mention anything about signing, Michaels."

David watched Ted's face turn a deeper red than usual. "Ted, nothing is going to be held against you if you sign this. It just shows to the others that you support what you see and that I received your input. It builds morale and commitment. After all, the information you gave me was accurate, wasn't it?" He offered a pen to Ted.

But Ted rebuked the offer. "Of course it was accurate. What kind of manager do you think I am? I have a reputation you know. A good one. And I plan to keep it that way. All right, give me the pen. I'll sign the thing." He grabbed the pen and signed the paper. He laid the pen on the table.

"Great. I'd also like you to review my version of the network diagram." David unfolded a large sheet on top of the work breakdown structure.

"The network what?"

"The network diagram. It simply shows the sequence of tasks and subtasks listed in our work breakdown structure," said David. "Right now, I'll only cover your portions. The way I've sketched it out, this task here precedes that one, and then this one happens."

David spent another 20 minutes discussing the accuracy of the network diagram.

"It's very clean. But by reconnecting some of those activity lines the way I mentioned you will find that the schedule, at least for my activities, will flow more smoothly. Do I need to initial this, too?" asked Ted. This time he patted David on the shoulder.

"Please," said David. He found it difficult to talk. Ted had never behaved this way before. He watched the man scribble his signature. "Thanks. Now there's just one more thing."

"What now?"

"Estimates. I need your estimates for how long each task will take." David knew he couldn't let this opportunity for cooperation pass.

"Are you kidding?" asked Ted. "I know estimates are important but you're asking for the impossible. There's no way I can be accurate. No way. A task could take 50 hours under the best of circumstances or 200 hours under the worst circumstances. I can't tell you which one is correct. It's impossible."

David saw Ted's facial muscles tighten. "Hold on, Ted. Remember, I said estimates. That means your best guess. An estimate means that you have a 50 per cent chance of being right."

"Yeah. And it also means that you have a 50 per cent chance of being wrong!"

"Look Ted, I need a gauge. I have an industry-proven formula that accounts for the best and worst amounts of time as well as a typical amount of time," said David.

"You do?" Ted cracked a smile. "OK, but this could take a long while."

David sensed that he was still in for a tortuous session. "I'm ready to take the time. But I need your help."

"You've got it. Let's get started," Ted said with a wave of his hand.

"Good. Now, looking at the first task, under the best of circumstances how long do you figure it will take?"

"In hours?" asked Ted. "Days? What?"

"Hours. Later, I'll convert the hours into days."

Ted gave a loud sigh and said, "Let's see . . . 72 hours, and that's if everything is in perfect order."

"How about under normal circumstances?" David grew impatient with Ted's eyes gazing about the room and his twiddling of the thumbs.

"About 100 hours."

"And under the worst circumstances?"

"Oh, let's see . . . 300 hours," said Ted.

"Great. Now, let's do each of the other activities." David then said, "It will take only 30 minutes. That is, if I have your complete attention. OK?"

Ted nodded his head and the two men began estimating how long to perform each task.

"That should do it," said David as he concluded the session. "There's valuable information here. It'll help me put a good schedule together."

"Tell me, am I the only person you're reviewing this with?"

"No, sir. I'm going to do the same with Sally, manager of the Animal Management Division, and Frank, manager for Administrative Services and Facilities Division," said David.

Ted pointed a finger at David. "I'll bet you dollars to doughnuts that there's going to be some disagreements over the schedule and the work breakdown structure. Whoops, I almost forgot about the network diagram thing. I'll bet lunch on that one, too."

"I'm looking forward to different reactions."

"You are?"

He wanted Ted to know that disagreement was positive. That was something he knew Ted could not tolerate. "I am. In fact, it's good. It will bring up issues early, not after the project has already begun," said David. "It's better to iron out our differences right at the start. I'd rather spend the time now than experience the pain later."

"Makes sense. Need me to initial the estimates?" asked Ted, smiling.

"Please. Thanks." He handed Ted the pen.

"Thank you. I don't have the fears about carrying out this project as I did with other projects. I guess it's because you forced me to see things through," said Ted.

"Same here. It's good stuff, and I know it works. Well, thanks for your help."

Ted rose from the table and extended his hand to David. With a tight grip, he shook the young executive's hand and left the office.

Now I've got to get the other two people's input, thought David. Then I've got to assimilate it into a schedule. It will take weeks just to calculate the dates for each task. There's got to be a faster way than doing it by hand. I'd better call Noah, after I've spoken to the other two people.

8

You need more than project management software to manage a project

◆

Pensively he sat at his desk. Should I? Yes? No? What the hell! He pulled a business card from his shirt pocket and turned it over and found the number he wanted. He pressed the buttons, Freephone–NOAH, on the phone.

"Noah, baby! Answer the phone. I need your help while I'm hot. Come on, Noah," David mumbled.

He heard a click on the other end of the line after the phone had rung several times. "Noah?" David's heart pounded.

"Yes."

"Thank God it's you. It's David." He took a deep breath. "I need some help. I did everything you said. I developed a statement of understanding, a work breakdown schedule, and a network diagram. I met with everybody individually and even got estimates. And signatures. I'm on a roll."

"That's good news. You're moving right along. Glad to hear it."

"There's still only one problem," said David.

"Only one, huh?"

"I need help."

A long dead silence followed. David started tapping his fingers on the desk.

"You've talked with a lot of experienced people and from what you've said I gather that you've gained their confidence and respect," said Noah. "So can't you and your team figure out some alternatives and pick the appropriate solution?"

"Of course I'm capable of solving my own problems. I'm a manager," said David.

"Is that 'manager' by title or by trade?" asked Noah.

"All right, all right. Look, just give me a clue, will you? You would be proud of me if you saw what I have collected so far," said David.

"I am proud of you. You've come a long way already. Just by culture shock. Anyhow, I know what your problem is."

"You do?" asked David. "I haven't even mentioned it yet."

"Now that you have all this wonderful data, what do you do with it?"

"Well, that's the problem. I collected a lot of data. The problem is displaying it clearly. And even before that, performing all those calculations, flowtime, start dates, stop dates. I'll be at it for days. How did you get your calculations done?" asked David. "I did some research about your Ark. You used about 750 truckloads of wood. It must have been one horrendous task to schedule pick-up, delivery, storage, and all the rest. So? How did you do it?"

Noah chuckled. "Mirrors, sonny. Mirrors."

"Mirrors?"

"And mechanical devices."

"And mechanical devices?" asked David.

"Stop repeating what I say and start thinking, David." I used mechanical devices to speed up my calculating process. The abacus was quite a useful tool in 2448 BC. But we're in a different era. It's the modern era. Different tools and all."

"This is the modern age? Big deal," said David.

"So make use of those available tools. You use current industrial technology to perform your assignments at work. You even use current industrial technology to get to work."

"Sure, I use automation to get to work. My four-wheel drive car has the latest anti-lock braking system and even tells me how much air is in each of the tyres," said David.

"What about at work?"

"At work? I have a microcomputer on my desk! What about it? I hardly use it though except for spreadsheets and word processing."

"Well David, why don't you expand your capabilities and use it for *work* processing?"

"Work processing?"

"Work processing," repeated Noah. "Use your computer to speed up your work and performance. For your project, you need to investigate the different types of project management software out there."

"You mean a project management software package for use on my personal computer? That's an excellent idea! But I don't have one on my computer," said David. "I don't even have any idea how in the world to use it."

"So learn. Learn by doing. It's called OJT or on-the-job training."

David saw a light bulb turn on in his head. "I could learn by using the tutorial that comes with a package. Most software nowadays comes with one. Or I could hire temporary help with that expertise. But I can't afford the latter. I guess I'll have to learn it myself. I can't wait to get started."

"How much computing experience do you have? You said you worked on spreadsheets and word processing before."

"Well, Noah, I type up my own memos. And I number-crunch our budgets."

"What do you know about project management?"

David fell back in his chair, shocked by the question. "What do you mean what do I know? You've taught me a lot. I'm not a recognized expert in the field, but I know enough to get started."

"And get stopped, too."

"*Touché*," said David.

"Listen. What's this wonderful package supposed to do for you? Do you have any idea?"

"Let's see . . . Calculate my flowtimes. Calculate my start and stop dates. If it does that much, it will save a lot of time," said David. "Oh, it has to print information, too, without a lot of aggravation. I've heard war stories of people trying to print out databases."

"I know most project management packages allow you to load in the names of tasks and subtasks, the dependencies between them, and each one's time duration. Then, the software calculates the start and completion dates. Then you can print schedules and diagrams. Some packages even let you perform resource loading. So you can see the relationship between time, people and dollars," said Noah.

"That's terrific. Makes sense. Real good sense. I'll leave right now and buy a package. I'm excited. Thanks for your help, Noah. You're a real life saver," said David.

"Not so fast, sonny."

"What's wrong? I don't understand," said David.

"You're right. You don't understand. What about requirements?"

"Requirements?" David let out a sigh. "I already told you what they are. You added a few good ideas, too, which I hadn't considered. Headcount, budgets – boy-oh-boy, this is going to be great."

"You're right, it will be great. But not until you've also identified your existing hardware. The world of hardware and software isn't always 100 per cent compatible," said Noah.

"You're telling me! It took me some time to figure out that the operating system I use wasn't compatible with the spreadsheet software I had purchased. Who knew? I was lucky that the store I bought it from exchanged it for me. But that's only because the owner's son was a friend of my cousin."

"You also need to know the contents of the schedules, reports, and diagrams you want to produce." Then Noah observed, "All software is not the same. And money? How much are you willing to spend for this wonderful software? More flexibility means more bells and whistles, meaning more money."

"Good point. I think I'll sit down and write down all my requirements . . . hardware . . . software . . . peripherals . . . even ergonomic features," said David.

"Good thinking."

"Once I have decided on the software, what should I do next?" asked David. A loud click over the line followed his question.

"Noah? Noah? Are you there? Sounds like he hung up on me. Maybe the connection went dead. But it sounded like he hung up." David redialled only to find the line was busy.

What do I do once I master the software? he thought. I know! I'll print a network diagram. Maybe even a bar chart. And a series of reports. I'll then send them to everyone to review and hold a group meeting to resolve any differences. Then, I'll revise accordingly. That's it!

9

A page of information is worth more than a book of data

◆

David pounded his fist on the office door. But he pounded with excitement, not anger. He couldn't wait to show off his new plans. He opened the door and stepped inside before getting any permission. "Mind if I come in?"

"I think you're already in. But come in anyway," said Harrison Farnsworth. "Haven't got much time, though. Got a lot of things going." He pointed to his cluttered desk. "What's the news?"

David helped himself to a seat next to Harrison's desk. "Plans. Good ones. I think your fears of 'plans don't get the job done' will be allayed."

"Better be good. I haven't seen much yet, other than the statement of understanding," said Harrison. He pulled out a cigar from his desk drawer and lit it.

"You will. First, here's a copy of the work breakdown structure," said David as he brushed aside the coarse cloud of smoke.

"That does look impressive. How did you get it to print out so neatly?"

David often wondered how his boss could see anything through the smoke. "Used a software graphics package on my microcomputer. You can see the box with the overall product and each of the deliverables shown underneath it. Beneath each deliverable are the tasks and, in some cases, subtasks."

"Fine, it looks nice. Thank you for the pretty picture. What else have you got there?" Harrison puffed harder on the cigar.

David knew that the intense puffing was common when his boss got excited. "A network diagram. This type of network diagram is called a precedence diagram. It shows the logical sequence of the tasks and subtasks. And the dates each should start and finish. Each box in the diagram represents an activity, and the arrows show the logical sequence."

"There's some additional information in the box. What's that for?" asked Harrison, pointing at the diagram.

"Oh yeah," said David. "That indicates the float, or slack time, for each activity."

"Float? Slack? What are you doing? Swimming around for answers? Or are you just slacking off?"

David caught the perplexed look on Harrison's face. "Hold onto your shorts a minute, boss, while I explain. Float or slack time is the amount of time that you can let a given activity slide without impacting the project's completion date. For the given activity it also shows the slack time of subsequent activities."

"I see. And the red line through the diagram?"

"That's the critical path."

"Critical path?"

"It's called the critical path, because that's what it is. Critical. This path shows you which activities you can't let slide without impacting the project completion date," explained David. "In terms of time, you must place your emphasis on those activities." David saw the confused look on his face disappear.

"I'm impressed. That's very useful information."

"Thank you, sir." David couldn't resist smiling. "But that's not all."

"Oh?"

"Here are some reports I generated on the computer. This report shows complete detailed schedule information for the entire project." David picked up another report. "This one shows tentative costs . . ."

"Slow down a minute," said Harrison. "These are nice looking and informative reports, but they show no figures. No dollars, no headcount."

David grinned like the cat that just caught the mouse. "That's right, because no people have been assigned to the activities in the schedule. I can assign responsibilities, but to whom? I have no manpower or budget. And without those items . . ."

"OK," said Harrison. He raised his hands as if to surrender. "I'm impressed with what you have done. I'll assign you some staff members right away. How many do you need?"

"Not so fast, sir," said David. "Good planning requires patience. I held one-on-one sessions with Ted, Sally, and Frank. Then I came up with what I've shown you today. It took me about two weeks. Now that you approve, I suggest that I hold a group meeting with all these folks again to get their consensus on what I've shown you here."

"But those people are the main team members that I was going to assign you. Why go back to them again? You went to them once already," said Harrison.

"I know, sir. But I need their consensus as a group. And together we can determine if the project is set up, as well as activities, interdependencies, and the like are stabilized. We can also determine if we have enough staff members, and not only that, but the right staff," said David.

"How are you going to figure that out?"

"I don't know. At least not yet."

"So what's your next step?"

"Action, sir!" David pounded his finger on the stack of papers. "I'm going to meet with the core team, as I call it, and get their consensus. Then the next step is to present you with the final plan, which will include cost and resource reports. That's what I'll do."

"Sounds logical to me. Well, I've got to get back to work as you can see from my desk. You seem to know where you are going."

David collected his stack of paper and headed towards the exit. But then he turned and said, "I know where I'm headed. I'm just not sure how I'm going to get there."

"You'll figure it out," assured Harrison. "That's why I hired you. I still have to say it. I'm impressed . . . so far. Doing this type of planning usually comes from someone with years of experience."

"You could say that again," said David as he closed the door behind him. "You could say that again."

10

Getting positive feedback is not all good; getting negative feedback is not all bad

◆

He sat before the group in the conference room, forcing himself to maintain a confident poise. Beneath the calm exterior sat a trembling young executive who wanted Noah by his side now more than ever before.

David cleared his throat and then spoke. "OK, folks. You've all had some time to review the work breakdown structure, the schedule reports, cost reports . . . let's see . . . the bar chart and the network diagram. In addition to having your own copy, I've posted them on the wall. Now, the purpose of this meeting is for us as a group, a team, to resolve any differences we may have concerning anything at all. And don't be shy. Realize, team, that even after our meeting things are subject to change."

"How could they change? We each gave you our best input," said Ted. He looked around as if trying to solicit a response from the others.

But none came.

Thank God, thought David. "You're right, Ted. Everyone did give their best input. Remember, though, that's for this time period. Right now. In a few days, a week, or even a month, things could change. And if they do, we want to catch those changes early," said David.

"Sort of like being adaptive," said Ted.

"Right," said David. "For instance, you could disagree over the way the work breakdown structure is set up. Or, the logic of the schedules. Even the estimates and the dates generated for starting and completing the tasks are subject to review. The aim here is getting everybody feeling confident about the game-plan that has been developed as a group and as a team."

"From my own perspective, the work breakdown structure looks great. There's just one thing I dislike in it," said Sally.

"What's that, Sally?" asked David.

"I don't like the order of the tasks."

Sally, having fiery red hair, was known for speaking her mind. She was somewhat on the chunky side, but still managed to turn heads when she walked by. She was loud and rarely, if ever, at a loss for words.

"Yeah, I don't like it either. What about you, Ted?" asked Frank.

Some people viewed Frank as the opposite of Sally. Soft-spoken, non-confrontational and agreeable were the hallmarks of his personality. He hated to argue and was once quoted as saying that the reason he didn't go into the navy was because he didn't like to make waves. He often went along with whatever Sally said.

"Looks fine to me," said Ted.

"Wait a minute," said David. He wanted to avoid any misunderstandings right away. "The order is insignificant. The work breakdown structure tells you only what has to be done, not in what order."

"Then what magic tells you the order?" asked Ted.

"The schedule. Remember?" asked David.

"Oh yes, that's right, Ted. David said it includes the tasks and subtasks listed in the work breakdown structure that can be exploded no further. Makes sense," said Sally.

"And the estimates?" asked Frank.

"What about them?" asked David.

"Where do the estimates come into play?" asked Frank.

"I took the estimates that you all gave me and translated the hours into flowtime, specifically days. I initially assumed an eight-hour working day," replied David.

"But many of the tasks shown in the network diagram will run concurrently. So how can we be in more than one place at a time?" asked Frank.

"You're right, Frank. You can't," said David. "That means I will have to do what is known as resource levelling. I need to make sure that the schedule accounts for the amount of hours, however limited, each of you will be available to work every day, and integrate that with the manpower currently available and then integrate that with what will be needed in the future."

"Do you want to do that here?" asked Sally. "Now?"

"We could, but I think it would take too long. What I would like to do is somehow profile the amount of time each of you and your people will be working on the project. Then I will meet with each one of you to get your concurrence. But right now, I need your concurrence on what I have here," said David.

"Looks good to me. Haven't seen this much planning in the 15 years I've been here. I feel comfortable about making this move happen. But I'm not comfortable about the prospect of losing my job," said Frank.

"I think the schedule looks great though I am a little concerned about the tasks looking so stacked up, one upon another. I'll sign off on the work breakdown structure and the estimates. But I won't sign off on the schedule until I see the results of your resource . . . what did you call it?" asked Sally.

"Levelling. Resource levelling," said David.

"I agree with Sally," said Frank.

"So it looks like the schedule needs to be modified," observed David.

"Not so much with the logic but the stacking of the tasks. Take my job, for instance. Three months down the road I will need to work 32 hours a day for ten days to complete four tasks that are run concurrently. My body, my mind, my 24 hour digital clock, just can't take that," said Sally.

"All right, folks, I understand your concern," reassured David. "I'll pass the other items around for your signature. Then I'll do the resource levelling. I'll make the revisions to the schedule and meet with everyone individually to get your feedback as to the changes. But does anyone here fundamentally disagree with the logic of the schedule? Which task begins first and occurs in parallel with others, the interdependencies and the like?"

"I must say, you did a hell of job planning this thing," said Sally.

"Yes, a superb job," added Frank.

Ted remained silent but nodded his head.

"Thank you for sharing your time with me," said David. "And for being committed to a team effort. We'll hold another team review in a few days. Got to run. I'm off to another meeting." David rose from the table. But before he could take one step he got another question.

"With whom?" interrogated Ted.

David thought for a few brief seconds. A smile came to his face as he moved to the exit. "A friend," responded David. "A very wise friend." He then disappeared.

11

Resource levelling doesn't necessarily mean chopping off heads

◆

David rested his elbows on the fence. He reached into a bag, removed a peanut, and gave it to the elephant.

You guys sure are lucky; your problems are peanuts in comparison to mine, he thought. He reached into the bag to get another peanut.

There was a tap on his shoulder. He turned and saw the old man. "Noah! Need to talk – I've got a problem."

"So what's new?" Noah took a deep puff from his porcelain pipe as he pushed back his blue cap.

"I've loaded all the data that I've collected so far into my project management software package," said David. "Now I have to make sure that I haven't overloaded my core team with work. There's only 24 hours in a day you know."

"That's a mighty long work day. I thought that eight hours was today's standard?" asked Noah.

"Stop with the jokes. I'm serious," said David.

"Lighten up. Resource levelling, that's your answer. You do some resource levelling, and you read the report which is in the form of a histogram. Smooth out the places where your team won't be able to perform due to excessive time considerations, and you're done," said Noah.

"A resource histogram? What does that look like?" asked David.

"Got a pen and paper?" asked Noah.

David gave him one from his pocket.

"Thanks. Give me a moment. There. Here's what one of my histograms looked like that was not level. It displays the number of people I needed for a six month time-frame. Notice that I needed between three and ten folks. And the sum of effort equalled 42 months."

"Now just one more moment," continued Noah as he scribbled on the paper. "There. Here's the same histogram, only levelled. And notice that its sum also equalled 42 months."

```
         ____10_____10____
          °       °       °
          °       °       °         ____7_____7____
          °       °       °       °       °
     ____5___     °       °       °       °
          °       °       °       °       °
  °       °       °       °       °       °
  °       °       °       °       °         ____3____
  °       °       °       °       °       °       °
  °       °       °       °       °       °       °

  °  Jan  °  Feb  °  Mar  °  Apr  °  May  °  Jun  °
_____
```

```
       7       7       7       7       7       7
  °       °       °       °       °       °       °
  °       °       °       °       °       °       °
  °       °       °       °       °       °       °
  °       °       °       °       °       °       °
  °       °       °       °       °       °       °
  °       °       °       °       °       °       °

  °  Jan  °  Feb  °  Mar  °  Apr  °  May  °  Jun  °
_____
```

"Notice the peaks and valleys in the unlevelled histogram?" David nodded his head.

"The peaks represent higher levels of work effort while the valleys represent lower levels. Hence, the higher the peak the more people per month I needed," said Noah. "That level of effort is indicated on the histogram."

"The levelled histogram looks better," observed David.

"Why?"

"Why?" asked David. It seemed so obvious. "Because you don't have to be so concerned about laying-off people or keeping them busy. You also optimize the use of their time."

"Good. Very good." Noah puffed on his pipe.

"I already know about resource levelling from my readings. The problem is actually how to make it happen like those histograms" said David.

"You have a team. You have tasks. You have work days. What more do you want?"

"I don't know how to make it all jive together," said David.

"It appears to me that you haven't loaded up everything as you claim."

"What do you mean I haven't loaded everything I need to into the computer?"

"Just what I said. I bet you didn't assign your people to their tasks. I also bet you didn't assign working days, and I do mean *working* days not holidays or vacation time, to your people either," said Noah.

"You mean I have to assign people to the tasks and also the number of days they work?" asked David. "I see — I think."

"Better think a little harder. Or read your project management software documentation a little better. You spent a lot of money on your off-the-shelf package. Now make it work for you," said Noah.

"So I need to enter who is to work on each task for a specific number of hours per day? That makes sense. That will generate costs for me, too. My package calculates costs based on our labour rates," said David.

"See? Money well spent. You just have to know how to use the software."

"I'll use the software, now that I understand how to use it," said David.

Noah chuckled and then took a deep drag from his pipe. A cloud of sweet-smelling smoke filled the air.

"That sure smells better than that stuff my boss smokes," noted David. "You know, making sure that no person works more than eight hours per day on the project unless absolutely necessary is hard. That is especially the case if activities occur concurrently. Right?"

David noticed that Noah gave no response but just listened while puffing away.

"So let's say that someone is working more than eight hours a day on the project. How do I go about reducing their time? What can I do?" asked David.

Still no response from Noah.

"Not even a hint?" asked David. He sighed. "That's why I'm talking to you, Noah. You have all the answers." Noah gave David a hard stare. "All right, all right. You're a tough old man! I'll work for the answers just like you did."

"Well, you could give it the old college try."

A response, thought David. He smiled. "You mean I could keep the schedule the way it is and hope that the person doesn't burn out or face any difficulties?"

"That's taking a chance. A calculated chance. And it's not stacked in your favour."

"You're right, that is taking a chance. I could reduce the number of hours per day to complete a task while extending the flowtime proportionally," said David.

"In the long run, that doesn't buy you much."

"You're right again," noted David. "I'd have to extend the flowtime of an activity that was not on the critical path. If I didn't make that distinction I could push out the project completion date by . . ."

"By a month or so. What's the big deal?"

"The big deal is I don't have that option. But I could reduce the hours that a person can work on a task and bring in more people to make up the difference," said David.

"More people means more lines of communication," exclaimed Noah. "More lines of communication means more concurrence. More concurrence means . . ."

"That it could cause problems. More people may slow productivity because they will need to overcome a learning curve and will make coordination more difficult. But adding people could be a possibility," said David.

"You could revamp the entire schedule. Start afresh."

"Yeah. I could also change the logic of the schedule. You know, reassign dependencies between activities. I could even re-estimate . . ."

"But that means going through the entire process of concurrence that you just completed."

David shook his head. "I'd hate to do that simply because I received the tacit approval from everyone concerning the schedule."

"Life's a challenge, eh?"

"Don't worry, I'm flexible. I'll consider all options," said David, turning away to feed the elephant standing behind him.

"Keep on thinking. You'll come up with the right answer."

"Noah, you've been a great help. Just answer one more question. Why did you hang up the phone on me?" He turned around.

Only a cloud of smoke remained where Noah had stood.

"Noah?"

12

Communicate!

S tacks of paper covered the top of the large round table. Both men gazed upon the documents while speaking.

"Here are all the components of my project plan. I think you'll be impressed," said David.

"Quite a bit of material here," observed Harrison as he started thumbing through the stack. "I've seen the statement of understanding. Here's the work breakdown structure . . . network diagram . . . let's see . . . labour utilization report . . . cost report showing the cost per activity and the entire project . . . schedule report displaying the duration, hours, start and stop dates, and float for each activity with accumulations shown at the bottom of the page . . . report showing who is assigned to what activities and the amount of effort."

David removed some papers from a manilla folder. "And I think you'll really like these." He handed the documents to his boss.

"Histograms showing resource utilization for each person working at the project. Interesting, no one is working overtime. Wait a minute . . ." Harrison puffed harder on his cigar, releasing an acrid smell.

"What?"

"Fred, one of Sally's people, is working 17 hours a day for two weeks. That's too much. And according to your histogram, Sally can't provide him any relief."

"You're right," agreed David. "I need to discuss bringing in additional help, at least temporarily. I've done all the levelling I could but can't do any more. We need one additional person to take up the slack."

"What about someone from Frank or Ted's area helping Fred?"

"Could do that. But no one else has Fred's skill."

"Good point. Well, I'll have to authorize additional help," said Harrison.

"Have I overlooked anything?" asked David.

"Not as far as I can see. In fact, in my 23 years in the business I have never seen such a well-planned project. I'm very impressed."

"Thank you, sir." David fought back the temptation to scream for joy.

"Have the others approved all this?"

"Everyone. Without exception. I held a follow-on team meeting prior to the one we're having now. I held it to get everyone's final approval of the histogram and the network diagram. They've each initialled all the documents in the upper right corner to indicate their agreement and support," said David, "as you can see." He pointed to a series of initials on the network diagram.

"Very good."

"I'd like your signature on them, too." David smiled.

"You bet. Now, it seems to me that these are good plans, but you need to do more."

"Such as?" David felt his smile disappear.

"Getting the word out about your plans and organizing them somehow. You have here a set of neat, well-crafted documents but somehow you need to organize it just a little better. A pile of paper will just be filed. You've made them legal, but now you have to give them the mark of distinction and an air of authority," said Harrison.

"You're right. I need to do something. I think I'd better make a phone call," said David.

"A call? To whom?" Harrison pulled the cigar from his mouth.

"To a friend. He's a great fellow. You can say he's been around for a long time and has a passion to help animals in distress," said David as he collected the pile of papers and placed them in his black leather attaché case. He then headed towards the exit.

"I'd like to meet him sometime."

"Oh, you have. You have, in an indirect way," said David with a big smile. He then softly closed the door behind him.

13

You can't operate as an organization without being organized

◆

D avid sat on a bench looking down at the gorillas from atop a small hill. Yeah, I'm pretty proud of myself. Fine job I did. Feel like one of those apes basking in the sun, thought David. He turned and spotted Noah. "Noah! You're right on time."

"How are things?" Noah lit his porcelain pipe as he sat down next to David.

David took a deep breath. He loved the smooth rich smell of Noah's pipe. "Fine. Just fine, Noah. You'd be proud of me. Everyone, including my boss, felt great about the planning I've done. I owe it all to you."

"So you developed a statement of understanding?" asked Noah.

"Yes, I did," replied David.

"Built a work breakdown structure from it?"

"I did that, too. In fact, I've done everything you suggested. Want to see the plans? I've got them in my attaché case here," said David.

"No. I believe you."

"OK. If you don't want to see them, that's fine with me," said David.

"You look surprised. And a little shocked."

"Well, I worked so long and hard. I thought you might want to see the fruits of my learning."

"I do want to see what you've done. But not until you've finished." Noah placed his arm around David's shoulder and gave it a squeeze.

"But I am finished," insisted David. "I did a network diagram, identified a critical path, have estimates . . ."

"You're finished with planning, but not done."

"You mean that it's not over?" asked David. "I don't understand."

"When we first talked, I mentioned that there were four secrets that lead to project success that I'd pass along."

"That's right. And I've learned only one of those four secrets."

"You want to learn the next one?"

"Of course I want to learn about the next secret. The first one was worth more than anything I could have ever imagined," said David. "So what is it?"

"None of your business. Asking, that is. You need to experience it for yourself."

"Oh. I see. You want me to arrive at the conclusion. Just like for the first secret, planning."

"That's right. It makes the secrets that much more valuable."

"So what do I do now that the plans have been developed? I suppose . . ."

"No suppositions. No prepositions. No dangling participles."

"I'm not taking this lightly, Noah. It's just that I'm enjoying the fruits of my labour. Planning is not easy, you know," said David. He grew impatient.

"You don't have to tell me about it. My Ark weighed in at about 25 million pounds. Unloaded. That averaged out to be 20 rooms per floor, with each room being 30 feet by 45 feet. You want to hear more?"

"All right, all right," said David, backing off. "I understand that I still have things to do. I realize I have all these plans put together . . ."

"How do you plan to communicate all that information?"

"I'll give everyone a copy," said David.

"First off, do you think everyone will read it? And secondly, do you think everyone will follow what's been written?"

"Of course, I realize that not everyone will follow it."

"So how do you figure on everyone going in the same direction? You have to align their thinking and actions somehow, don't you? Otherwise you're going to have a hard time completing your project," said Noah. He took a deep puff. A cloud of sweet-smelling smoke encircled his head.

"What you're telling me is that I have to set up some mechanisms to ensure that everyone knows what the project is about and what the plan is to implement it."

"How are you actually going to do that?"

"Well, I could compile planning documentation and other useful information."

"How about a project manual?"

"A project manual?" asked David. "Yes, that's it. I could do that. I could divide it into sections. For instance, a section for the plans. Another for listings, like phone numbers and addresses. Still another section could contain procedures to follow throughout the project. I could even have a miscellaneous section. Did you have a manual, Noah?"

"You bet I did, sonny!"

"I think you know my next question," said David.

"All right, I'll sketch the outline of my project manual. Just for you," said Noah. He laid his pipe on the bench, and pulled out a pen and a folded sheet of paper from his pocket. Then he started writing. "Here's what its basic structure looked like."

PROJECT MANUAL

1. Introduction
2. Executive Summary
3. Scope
4. Goals/Objectives
5. Planning
6. Implementation
7. Organization
8. Work Breakdown Structure
9. Administrative/Operating Procedures
10. Schedules
11. Meetings/Reviews
12. Finance/Resource Requirements
13. Contractors
14. Miscellaneous

"Now I have a question for you, David. Will everybody get a copy?"

"You bet. I'll give a copy to each person on the project."

"Great. But you still haven't addressed responsibilities. You know, who is supposed to do what."

"That's another problem," observed David. "I just don't know how to communicate responsibilities effectively. Wait a minute. A matrix! I'll put together a matrix showing which person has responsibility for completing which tasks. Tell me, Noah, what did your responsibility matrix look like?"

Noah laid a white box of popcorn flatly on his lap and began sketching on it. "My responsibility matrix looked something like this."

RESPONSIBILITY MATRIX

DESCRIPTION	RESPONSIBILITY			
	NOAH	SHEM	HAM	JAPHETH
1.1 Identify requirements	X			
1.2 Draft plan		X		
2.1 Prepare specifications	X		X	
2.2 Establish design	X	X		X
3.1.1 Fashion keel	X	X		
3.1.2 Lift keel onto blocks	X	X		
3.1.3 Bolt floors to keel	X			X
3.1.4 Attach stem to keel		X	X	X
3.1.5 Attach sternpost to keel			X	X
3.1.6 Attach keelson to floor		X	X	
4.1 Obtain supplies	X	X	X	X
4.2 Gather animals	X	X	X	X
5.1 Make modifications		X	X	

"How will everyone on your project get a copy of the matrix?" asked Noah.

"I can place a copy in the project manual. That'll work, for sure. Anything else?" asked David.

"I know that talking with people helps, so you might want to consider . . ."

"Meetings? Good idea," said David. "But when should I have meetings?"

"There is more than one type of meeting. There's . . ."

"I know," interrupted David. "I could have a meeting after the completion of each major deliverable."

"There you go. A checkpoint review meeting."

"A what?" asked David. "Sounds like something at the Berlin Wall."

"Wrong. You conduct this type of meeting to verify that what was supposed to be done has been done, before proceeding further. You might also consider holding status meetings."

"A superb idea. I was going to mention it myself. I'll have a status meeting every week. I think I'll have it on Fridays. In it, I'll assess the status of completion on each item in the schedule and make decisions regarding future actions," said David.

"Sounding good." Noah took a deep puff from his pipe and released a cloud of purple smoke.

"So, there you have it. I'll have two sets of meetings. One at the conclusion of each set of activities that will produce a deliverable, and one each week to collect and assess status." David took a deep breath and asked, "So, am I through?"

"Not yet."

"What do you mean I'm not through? I don't quite understand. I'm putting together a project manual, a responsibility matrix, and holding meetings. What else is there to do?" asked David.

"Know thy boss. Know his domain."

David said, "Look, Noah, I don't know who you report to but I have to report to someone else."

"I knew my hierarchy's pecking order. Do you know yours?"

"You report to God," said David. "Well, I have to report to a higher power, too. We all report to somebody."

"That's my point, sonny."

"Why, you old sneak. You're leading me to the conclusion that I need to develop an organization chart. What a grand idea. I bet you didn't have one."

"Oh yes I did," said Noah. He reached down from the bench and pulled up a large piece of brown cardboard about the size of a standard hard-cover text book. He drew an organization chart. "Here's what mine looked like."

"The way I figure it, I have 21 people supporting me from a total of three divisions," said David.

"What about appointing leads?"

"Appointing what? Leads? For only 21 people?"

"Yes. You can delegate work to a lead who in turn will delegate to other members on the team. This will leave you free to do other things."

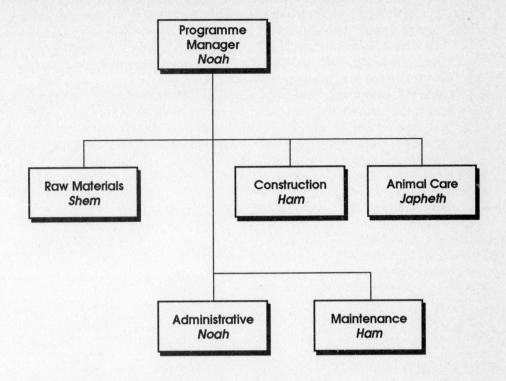

Figure 13.1 Organization chart

"But I don't have any leads now and everything is going fine."

"How are you fixed for time to manage them when you start implementing your plans?"

"I'll admit I sometimes have a tough job managing them now," said David. "I sometimes find it hard to keep track of what they're doing and how well they're doing it. That is in addition to performing my own assignments."

"Are you familiar with the term 'span of control'?"

"Span of control?"

"As a manager, you can only effectively manage up to seven people reporting directly to you. Otherwise you can get too caught up in administrative tasks and not have enough or even any time left to accomplish your own tasks," said Noah.

An idea came to David. "Based upon that definition, I could split my team into three sections, each having a lead. I can appoint each of my core team members leads. That would make my job easier. And I'd be more productive."

"So you'll need some means of telling everyone who's who in the zoo?"

"You're right, I'll need to let everyone know who is reporting to whom. I can produce an organization chart. That will show the reporting relationships. Noah, you're a Godsend."

"Now you've uncovered the second secret." Noah rubbed the end of his pipe like someone rubbing a bottle to release a genie.

"I have?" asked David. "So what's the secret? Or have I missed it?"

"You haven't missed it; you're right on it. Organizing."

"Organizing?" David felt his blood race through his veins. "That's it?"

"It's a big IT, not a small one."

"I'm getting my act together! Once I build a project manual, set dates for my meetings, and publish an organization chart, I'll have effectively established a means for communicating with my team members and my management. I'll also develop a formal structure of tasks and relationships," said David.

"You're on a roll, but you're not done yet."

"More?" David shook his leg back and forth.

"More to come, really. I'm getting kind of tired. I've had a long day. Let's continue at another time. OK?" Noah emptied the contents of his pipe onto the ground and stepped on the ashes.

"Tired? Another time? When? Noah, don't leave. I have more questions. Noah . . ." pleaded David.

But Noah disappeared in the crowd as fast as David jumped to his feet. "Noah," he mumbled, "sometimes I get the impression that you think I can handle this project all on my own."

14

Communicating your plans is as important as making them

◆

David whistled to the music from the radio as he worked, standing up, at a table covered with papers and three-ring binders.

"Come in, Harrison," said David as he placed papers into binders. "What the hell are you . . ."

"Just getting organized," said David.

"I would never have guessed. You've got paper spread out everywhere."

"I'm putting together a project manual."

"A what?" Harrison moved closer.

"A project manual. What I'm doing is taking a three-ring binder and some dividers. Then, I label each divider by a topic. Looks really sharp. I'm not finished with this one, yet. I'll be giving a copy to all team members." David handed his boss a binder. "Here's one that's done. It's your copy."

"Looks like a lot of administrivia to me." Harrison ruffled a few papers. "A bunch of paperwork. I told you before that we don't have a lot of time to . . ."

"Sir, just take a minute to look at what's there. I think you'll get a different impression."

"All right. I'll give you the benefit of the doubt. Besides, I encouraged this because I was impressed with what I saw so far. Let's see, here is the table of contents page."

"Pretty impressive, eh?" asked David.

"I should say so! Complete project plan, listings, responsibility matrix, organization chart, miscellaneous section. I'm damned impressed. Who else gets a copy of this project manual?"

"Everyone on the team," replied David. "It's a good reference manual for them."

"Who will update it?" Harrison continued to ruffle through the pages.

David started to put another book together as he spoke. "I'll update it. But if I get overloaded, I'll delegate the responsibility to someone who is not working on a critical path task. That should solve that."

"This manual is like a bible."

"What a coincidence," said David.

"What?"

"Oh, nothing," said David. "It's just that when you compared it to a bible, you reminded me of someone. That's all."

"I see. Tell me, you've got a lot of information contained in this manual. It's neatly organized. I notice in the section on meetings that you have two types of meetings."

"That's right, the checkpoint review meeting and the status review meeting."

"I read their descriptions. You stated that at each meeting there must be an agenda, identified in advance."

"You bet. That's so every meeting stays on course," said David.

"And you say that each meeting should not exceed two hours?"

"That's right, too," added David. "I don't want the people spending a lot of their time at a meeting and not conducting direct work for the project. Just a little psychological mechanism to keep meetings from turning into bull sessions."

"Excellent. I like that. I might even take that approach with my own meetings. I did notice, however, that you lacked one other type of meeting."

He stopped what he was doing and looked at his boss. "I did? What?" asked David.

"The staff meeting."

"Of course, I should have known." David slapped his forehead. "The staff meeting. You're right. I need to have one just to discuss general issues about the project. Issues that don't reflect the status of the project. That would give me an opportunity to impart information to team members. And it would give the team an opportunity to raise issues not concerning status. It also improves communication, morale, and team clearing."

"What's team clearing? I never heard of that term before. Is it one of those fancy MBA words you learned in college?"

"Team clearing brings out in the open any emotional feeling one has about the project, team, activities, or dynamics that have an adverse reaction to positive synergy."

"Right. Now I noticed one other thing."

"What?" asked David. If it's not one thing it's another, he thought.

"Don't get defensive, now. I'm impressed with all this. I noticed that you do not have a list of attendees at each type of meeting," said Harrison. He turned to a page in the manual and pointed to it. "I'm sure the list is different for each type of meeting. Why have someone there who doesn't need to be there? And why omit someone who should be there?"

"Excellent point, sir. I'll make a listing for each meeting. Makes good sense. Thanks, boss. Didn't mean to sound defensive. It's just that it seems that there are mounds of details," said David, revealing a smile.

"I'll tell you what. What you've done so far helps you tremendously in keeping account of all those mounds. I wish I had done this type of planning and organizing on projects that I previously conducted. I would have had less grief." Harrison headed towards the door but stopped just before it.

"Thanks," said David.

"So what's next?" asked Harrison as he opened the door.

"I have to distribute the manual. But before I do so I have to see someone — I mean do something — before I give them out." David resumed filling a three-ring binder.

"What's that?" asked Harrison.

David smiled and said, "Let me just say some things that will help me . . . stay afloat."

"Same here. I've got things to do myself. Keep up the good work," said Harrison as he closed the door behind him.

15

You can produce quantity without quality

◆

Strolling through the zoo with a copy of the project manual under his arm, David approached an old man whose back was turned away from him. The man's long grey hair and Greek fisherman's cap told him it could be only one person. "Noah."

The old man turned around, looked up and said, "Hi, sonny."

"I haven't eaten all day. Walk me over to the refreshment stand, will you?" asked David. "I'll buy you a hot dog and a coke."

"I'm a vegetarian. How about a float? A root beer float with vanilla ice-cream. It sure is hot outside today."

"OK, I'll buy you that instead."

"What's that you've got tucked under your arm? You weight lifting?"

David handed the book to Noah. "It's my project manual. I'd like you to take a look at it."

Noah scanned through the pages and gave back the book. He lit his pipe and said, "It looks good, but there's something lacking."

"What's wrong? Something missing? I really spent a lot of time figuring it out, putting it together, and . . ."

"I know you did. You were pretty thorough. But, for me, I like examples. Forms with real life examples that are related to your project would be nice." Noah puffed on his pipe.

"Forms?" asked David. Not another oversight, he thought. There's got to be a limit to these damn oversights.

"Yes. Samples of forms and accompanying instructions addressing the who, what, when, where, and how of their administration."

"I understand that forms are important for getting organized. But isn't that overkill?"

"Overkill? Look, David, if I gave you a job to do, you would do it?"

"That's right, Noah."

"And how long would it take you?"

"What kind of question is that? It depends on the job."

"That's right," assured Noah. "But let's say that I gave you a written description with a picture of what I wanted to be accomplished. Wouldn't it take you less time to complete the job?"

"Yes it would."

"That's because you'd have a clearer understanding of what was required. And that's the purpose of forms. Forms can also become standard operating procedure, so nobody has to re-invent the wheel," said Noah.

"All right, I'm sold on the idea. But what types of forms do I need?" asked David.

"I give up! Tell me."

"OK, I'll try to figure it out myself," snapped David. "I'll need a form for collecting status on the progress of each activity in the project. That's when each activity starts and finishes and their percentage completion during that timeframe."

"That's it?"

"You think I need another?" asked David.

"What about areas that you're concerned about that are related to, but not specifically identified in, your project plan?"

"You mean some mechanism that records problems that need to be addressed but are not part of the project plans?" asked David.

"Another form, perhaps?"

"I could develop a form that would account for problems," said David. "That way, I can capture all the information to resolve the issues that arise as they arise."

"Good. You might consider yet another form."

"Another? Wait . . . I'll create a form to capture requests for changing the schedule, budget, and ways of carrying out the project. You know, a change control log." David smiled.

Noah released a huge cloud of purple smoke. "You're not done yet. What about purchased items?"

"For purchases, huh?" asked David as he enjoyed the aroma. "Then, I'll put together a purchase order form. There's probably already one in existence for the zoo. I'll use that one. I don't like re-inventing the wheel myself."

"You work. Your team works. What about a form that captures . . ."

"Labour utilization. Got an idea for that, too. I'll put a form together that keeps track of all labour used on a daily basis. I'll use it for contractors only."

"Now that you have a form for labour utilization, how about one for non-labour utilization?"

"Non-labour utilization? You mean like renting forklifts and wrecking equipment?" asked David. "Great idea. I'll produce a form for that."

"Maybe the zoo already has one. There's a pattern that you're generating, here."

"I see it. I need a set of forms that address schedule, budget, and quality. Smart. Real smart. Well, I guess that about does it?" asked David. Please say yes, he thought. Just a little mercy, please.

"Poor guess, sonny. You'll need to report on what you're doing."

"Reports? You think I need a portfolio of reports?"

"Yes, and instructions on how to interpret them."

"You're right. I'm sure that I will need reports that address the three areas you just mentioned: schedule, budget, quality."

"What kinds of reports will you need for them? Start with the schedule."

David nodded his head, less out of agreement than for surrendering to the onslaughts. "All right. I'll compile a report that lists each activity, giving the planned and actual start and finish dates and remaining duration for those activities not finished or started, and float. The report will also give estimated completion dates, based upon planned and actual progress of all activities and for activities that remain unfinished, and an estimated completion date for the entire project."

"Anything else?"

"You're asking me? Well, I can also produce a bar chart or a network diagram, or both, showing the per cent complete for each activity."

"Good. Now for the budget."

"As for budget, I have an answer there, too. I'll produce a report that lists the planned and actual monies spent for each activity and for the entire project up to the time that the report was generated. It will also include a projection of what will be spent for each activity when one hundred per cent complete. It'll also have a projection for when the entire project is one hundred per cent complete. And I'll do similar reports for labour utilization," said David.

"Let's get on with quality now."

"Ah. With regards to quality, I'll produce a summary listing of all problems identified in both the problems form and the change control forms. This summary report will list when each occurrence happened, its description, its current status, and a projected date of resolution," said David. "How's that?"

"Great. Now that you have these wonderful reports, what are you going to do with them?" Noah started blowing smoke rings in the air.

"Hmm . . . I put all this material in the project manual. I knew that something was missing, but I didn't know what. To tell you the truth, Noah, I guess I really didn't need to talk with you after all. It seemed that I had all the answers already. I only had to discuss them aloud," said David.

"Then why bug me? I have other things to do, too, you know. Or haven't you thought of that?"

"Now, Noah, don't get sensitive," said David. He looked up at the sun and got blinded. By the time he regained his eyesight Noah was gone. "Where did you go? You haven't left me for good, have you? Noah?"

16

Sometimes there's little trivia in administrivia

◆

All the team members huddled around a long, narrow mahogany table. David sat at the front of the table sandwiched between two overhead projectors. In front of everyone on the table was a white binder.

"I am glad everyone of you could attend this kick-off meeting for our project," said David with a serious look on his face. "In front of you is a three-ring binder. It is your copy of the project manual. In it, you will find the information you need to work on our project."

"Does it have the work breakdown structure we developed?" asked Ted.

"It certainly does," replied David.

"And the schedule?" asked Sally.

"That's right."

"What about good reference material, such as a phone listing and an equipment listing?" asked Frank.

"It's all there, just about everything you'll ever need."

"I've got a problem," said Ted.

"What's that?" asked David.

"No offence, buddy, but this manual represents to me nothing more than a bunch of administrative red tape. The more time I take to read through this jumbo, the less time I have to do real work. And I have a lot of real work to do – and so do the rest of us," said Ted.

David sat silent with a look of surprise on his face.

"That's right, red tape," continued Ted. "Look. You've got diagrams . . . charts . . . listings . . . forms . . . reports . . . It's full of paperwork. I'll be concentrating more on the paperwork rather than the job."

"Yes, come to think of it, he's right," added Sally.

"I agree," said Frank.

"Now wait a minute, folks. Don't jump to any conclusions," said David.

"How's that? I mean, just because we get a manual about the thickness of Moby Dick doesn't mean anything, right everybody? What's it worth, anyway? It looks professional, so what?" persisted Ted with a look of sarcasm.

David fought to keep cool. "It's reference material. That's all. Sure you'll have forms to complete. That's involved in just about every project. And yes, you will receive reports. But that's about it. Look at it from this standpoint, Ted. Say you wanted information regarding how to order some equipment to complete a task, what would you normally do?"

"I'd try to find the appropriate form, complete it, and submit to whomever processes it. I'd probably have to ask someone like Fred for the information," said Ted.

David smiled and said, "You just proved my point."

"How's that?" asked Ted. His face became crimson as he took a deep swallow.

"You'd have to reduce your amount of productive time to find the form and process it. In addition, you'd have to interrupt someone else, possibly Fred, in order to get the answer. So now two people lose productive time," explained David. *Touché*, he thought.

"Yes, but my time may not be that significant," said Ted.

"I'll agree with that," said Sally with a laugh.

Frank raised his hand and spoke. "Yes, but if the entire team reduces their productive time in order to handle administrative tasks, then cumulatively that turns into a significant amount. And what about forms that haven't been created yet? Then what? More re-inventing the wheel. And not only that, but everybody will spend time making up their own. That's duplication of effort. So more productive time is being lost."

"Good point, good point," said Ted.

"I rest my case," said Frank. "But who's going to maintain it?"

"I'll answer that in a minute." David saw Sally give soft applause and then said, "I specifically chose this conference room because it has two overhead projectors." He pointed to one projector and then the other. "On one projector I'm going to show the network diagram and on the other I'm going to show the responsibility matrix. All the material I'm going to show up on the screens is included in the project manual."

"So we can all be looking at the same thing at the same time. That eliminates a lot of confusion. Good thinking," said Sally.

"Thank you. Look at the network diagram on the screen on the right. The line in red indicates the critical path. Now look at the activities on the responsibility matrix. Who is not on the critical path?" asked David.

"I'm not" said Frank.

"That's right. So, you get to upkeep the manual," said David. "That answers your question as to who is going to upkeep the manual."

"Thanks a lot," said Frank.

"It's more important than you might think, Frank," said David. "We, the whole team, need to be working from the same set of forms, reports, and instructions. Your job helps to keep us honest. Ted and Sally, you two are working on the first activity. And it's on the critical path. The start date is today and it must be finished in three weeks. Is there anything you need to complete the activity? Do you have any concerns?"

"We need some technical advice, preferably from engineers. We don't have the procedures necessary to dismantle some of the animal confinement areas without hurting the animals," said Sally.

"That's a good point," added Ted. "We've never had much experience with this issue."

"Why don't you contact the engineering firm that we have on retainer to see what advice they can give? I have their number. See me after the meeting. Now, do you see the value of all this?" asked David.

"Sure, sure. There's just one other problem here, David," said Ted.

"What's that?"

"How are we going to keep track of how well we are working, according to your plans?"

"A good question, Ted. But remember that it's *our* plans, not just mine. You signed-off on them. See your signature on the schedule? We're all in this boat together."

"I know I signed," said Ted with a sigh. "And so did the others."

"Good. If there are no further questions, I'll see you at our first status review meeting in four days. I'll send you each an agenda for that meeting tomorrow. Until then," added David, "let's keep up the good work."

David then left the conference room, only this time with a smile on his face.

17

Spare no detail but keep an overall perspective on the project

D avid pressed the digital buttons on his office phone. It rang for a long
time before someone answered.

"Noah? Is that you?"

"Yes it is," said Noah.

A wide grin came to his face. "Man alive, I've been trying to get hold of you
for a week."

"I've been out."

"I was worried that you got angry and decided not to help me any more. It's
really good to hear your voice." Thank you, Lord, David thought as he looked
up to the ceiling.

"So, tell me what you know."

"You mean what have I learned so far? Well, a lot," said David.

"A lot of what? Jargon?"

"I'm not being smart, Noah," said David. "I'm being truthful. You've really
taught me a great deal."

"Is that so? Then it's quiz time. Give me an overview of your project's
progress."

"Sure, Noah. I'll give you an overview. So far, I've learned two secrets."

"What are they?"

"I'm getting to them. I learned first that I need to plan before acting on the
project."

"And the other?"

"Now, wait a minute, Noah. Let me finish," said David. He took a deep
breath. "Remember, you taught me about patience. Now, planning involves
taking several actions. I have to develop a statement of understanding which
explains at a high level what must be accomplished, what major tasks to
perform and any constraints I face, and the support I will need. Then I can
develop a work breakdown structure."

"And what's the work breakdown structure?"

"You bet I know what it is. It's a listing of tasks exploded from a general level to one of more specific detail. Using the work breakdown structure, I build a network diagram. It shows the logical relationships among tasks."

"You also use it to determine start and stop dates, and . . ."

"That's right, Noah. You use it to calculate the start and stop dates as well as the float for each task. Of course, you will need to have the estimates for how long it will take to complete each task."

"And the critical path?"

"Of course I know what the critical path is. It's the path through the network diagram that cannot slide past its estimated completion date without impacting the overall project's estimated completion date," said David.

"I'm satisfied."

David waved his arms as he wedged the receiver between his head and shoulder. "Glad you're satisfied. Now for a review of your second secret, organizing."

"Go right ahead."

"It involves putting in place mechanisms for effective communications and establishing a formal structure of tasks and authorities."

"What textbook did you get that definition from?"

"No, I didn't read that from some textbook. I learned it from you," said David.

"I must be smarter than I thought. What does it entail?"

"It involves developing a project manual," explained David. "Setting up different types of meetings. Preparing and distributing an organization chart. Building a responsibility matrix. In other words, getting your act together."

"It seems to me that you've got it down. You're seeing the total picture."

"Now, Noah, you said that there are four secrets. You've proven to me that the first two work. I'm game for the other two," said David. Please tell me, Noah, he thought. He wanted to know even if it meant getting down on his hands and knees.

"I think you're smart enough to figure it out for yourself."

Somehow I knew he'd say that, David thought. "I understand. You want me to discover the other two. Fine, what's the third one?"

"I tell you to discover the others by yourself: you say you understand, but in the same breath you ask me what the third one is! I can't tell you now."

"Why won't you tell me over the phone? It's not top secret is it?"

"There are certain things I just don't like sharing over the phone."

"OK, you win. How about in the zoo in an about an hour?" asked David.

"How about in 73 hours?"

"You mean in an hour and three days. At the zoo? I don't understand . . ."

"Your project is underway, isn't it?"

"Sure the project has started, but . . ."

"Let's spend time together when you have some difficulties to overcome," said Noah. "Right now I'm busy."

"Wait until I get flooded with problems?" asked David.

"That's right, then call me." Noah hung up.

Noah, why do you hang up and leave so abruptly? thought David.

18

Are you managing changes or are they managing you?

◆

The door swung open and slammed against the wall. Harrison barged into David's office.

"What's wrong?" asked David.

Harrison wrung his hands as a grimace covered his face. "Everything, everything."

"Sit down," said David, pointing to a chair next to his desk. "You look really rattled."

"I should. You will be, too, after I get through telling you the deal." Harrison sat down.

"Let me guess. We're getting fired," said David.

"No. Not yet anyway," said Harrison. "I just received word from Craig Yuggenheim. He and his family want to complete the project two months earlier than planned. And with half the staff. He's also cutting the monies appropriated for the project by ten per cent on top of the reduction in manpower costs. I'm telling you, this is crazy." He threw up his hands.

"My God. We haven't even gone through a whole month on the project and already disaster strikes," said David.

"There's one other problem."

"What's that?"

"Well, David, I showed him your set of plans. I must say he was quite impressed. Really liked them."

"Great."

"But it's not as good as you might think."

"What do you mean?" David had never had a compliment that gave bad tidings.

"He wants to see your plans for the changes that I just mentioned. He wants them real soon."

"But . . ."

"I mean in two days. That's how soon. Otherwise, he'll consider other options."

"What does that mean?" David asked. But he knew the answer.

"Terminating our working relationship immediately and having the animals slaughtered."

"What?" asked David. "He can't do that. He'll never get away with it."

"Oh? Who says?"

"Animal activists. And there are other groups."

"Look, enough of the emotional outbursts. We've, no *you've* got some heavy duty thinking to do."

"That's what I like about you: your ability to get right to the heart of the matter," said David.

"I've been around a lot longer than you. And I've been through a lot more."

"Why did they change the deadline?" asked David. "I don't understand?"

"Money. The Habeas Corporation offered 25 per cent more for the zoo grounds if the Yuggenheims delivered two months earlier."

"Wow, that's quite an incentive. But I don't know how we're going to adapt to these circumstances, boss."

"You'd better, kid. Use your planning skills. Use your organizing skills. Use all your skills. You used them before, you'd better use them now. Well, got to go." Harrison jumped to his feet and walked out of the room.

David never felt so alone, abandoned. "Noah, I'm calling you again whether you like it or not," mumbled David. He picked up the receiver and dialled Freephone–NOAH. The phone seemed to ring forever.

"Hello."

David recognized the voice. "Look, Noah, I know we just talked. But I need to talk with you right away. And not on the phone. Can we meet somewhere?"

"Oh, all right. How about at the zoo?"

"Where in the zoo?"

"Not by the monkeys."

"How about by the elephants? I'll bring a snack. One of your favourites, animal cookies," said David.

"And some cold milk, too, please."

"Noah, you never cease to amaze me. See you in 30 minutes?"

" 'Bye."

David heard the familiar click. "Great. Noah, you're a Godsend!" he said.

19

Minimize the pain; maximize the gain

Noah was sitting on a bench smoking his pipe while watching the elephants lounge in the sun.

"There you are," said David. He sat next to Noah. "Glad you could make it."

"Nice day out here," said Noah, pushing back his fisherman's cap and packing the tobacco in his pipe and lighting it. The familiar sweet-smelling cloud of smoke hovered above.

"Look, I know you're busy and so am I. I'd like to get straight to the point," said David. He pulled from a brown bag he was carrying a small milk carton and a box of animal crackers.

"I see. Just what is the point?" Noah grabbed the food and placed his pipe on the bench and started feeding himself.

"Well, my boss just hit me with a bombshell," said David.

"Sounds more like a target than a point. You getting laid off?" asked Noah with a mouthful of food.

"No, I'm not getting fired," said David with a sigh. "But the potential is there. The Yuggenheim family is interested in negotiating a deal with the Habeas Corporation."

"Is that so?"

"The family wants to move the final completion forward by two months," said David.

"Is that it?"

"No, that's not all," said David. "They also want to reduce the staff to half its current size."

"Is that it?" asked Noah.

"Glad you're taking it so lightly, Noah. There's more. They also want to reduce expenditures by an additional ten per cent. I have to put 'new' plans together within two days. These plans will then be presented to Craig Yuggenheim, the head of the business."

"Think positive. You'll be getting some great visibility." Noah wiped the milk and crumbs from his chin. He then put his pipe back in his mouth.

"Don't be facetious. Now you know why I need to talk with you right away," said David.

Noah gave David the empty milk carton and box of animal crackers. "Not really. Have you learned anything from this experience?"

"What do you mean, have I learned anything from this?" I came here to learn from this experience, he thought. He crushed the milk carton and box with his hands. It seemed to release the tension inside him.

"What I'm speaking of is contingency planning. That's what a back-up plan is. A contingency just in case something unexpected crops up. Your project is a good example of where a contingency plan is quite helpful," said Noah.

"It was totally unexpected, though. It completely caught me off guard."

"Did you ever duel? With swords I mean?"

"Fencing? You mean fencing? No I haven't."

"There's a special term in fencing meaning 'assume the position for action' and it's just one word. *Engarde*. And you, dear sonny, were off guard, not on guard," lectured Noah. "Plan for the unexpected. Like what would you do if your computer suddenly blew up and you lost a whole month's work? Or how about your car, the one that tells the air pressure in every tyre. What would happen if one morning it wouldn't start?"

"That's easy. I'd either get a friend to drive me or I'd take a bus."

"There's your contingency plan for the automobile. How about for the computer?"

"I never thought of that."

"Better start."

"All right," said David, shaking his head. "I accept the fact that I should have developed some type of contingency plan. So, I made a mistake. I won't let it happen again. I'll follow the old English proverb that says hope for the best but prepare for the worst."

"There you go."

"Tell me, Noah, now that I've learned from the errors of my ways, how do I go about replanning?" David tossed the milk carton and box of animal crackers into a nearby waste basket.

"Before you start replanning, you must first look at change management," said Noah. A rare smile came to his face. "For example, when a baby's clothes get soiled, they must be changed. The replanning is to get clean clothes on. Change management, however, involves procedures necessary to implement effectively that change to clean clothes."

"Change management? I don't get what's so important about that" said David. "We develop different plans and everyone follows them. That's all there is to it."

"Just because it's written down and supported by upper management is no guarantee that it will be followed to the letter. Or even followed at all. Change affects the way people feel. Let me give you an experience I had on the Ark," said Noah.

"This should be interesting."

"It will and also illustrate the need for change management."

"So start."

"Speaking of soiled laundry, we too, on board the Ark, had a means of recycling our refuse," said Noah. He took a deep puff of his pipe. "Since our supplies were confined to that which was on board, we were interested in saving and salvaging as much waste material and by-products as possible. And we wrote down a procedure to do that.

"However, on-the-job training convinced us otherwise," continued Noah. "It was more productive to throw away certain scrap rather than to sift through the spent material and try to keep what was useable. And we never changed our original rules. We felt good that we improved efficiency. Nevertheless, we neglected to keep our paperwork current with our procedures. And one day this almost got us into a heap of trouble. God asked us why we were doing it 'that' way. We told Him of our improved method. He told us that next time He'd like to be aware of such decisions, and left it at that. We felt relieved. But not every boss is that flexible."

"I see," said David, shaking his head. "Change can impact the way people feel about themselves, their job, and their company."

"Change affects schedule, budget, and quality. Let's start off with schedule."

"The schedule?" asked David. "A change in the schedule could accelerate work, meaning you have to do more work in a shorter period of time. Or if the end date is extended, the time to do the work will lengthen. Either way, such change impacts productivity, negatively or positively."

Noah pointed his finger skyward. "A shorter period of time can result in people working overtime. That can mean people getting tired, morale drops, and productivity declines. A longer time period can mean people get a chance to drag their feet. What about budget?"

"Budget?" asked David. "Well . . . increasing the budget does not necessarily mean better productivity. It may mean money to burn. Less money may result in lower productivity because people do not have the right tools to do their jobs efficiently or effectively."

"And quality?"

"Changing the level of quality can have an impact," explained David. "If you increase quality it could result in an increase in expenditures or a delay in meeting the schedule. Lowering quality can result in disaster, especially in the long run, such as considerable rework or lawsuits."

"Lesson learned?"

"What's the lesson from this? That change can have a positive or negative impact. That's the lesson."

"Any others?"

"Another lesson?"

"How about changing the rules and not telling anybody that a change is going to take place? How would you feel when change day comes around, and you didn't even know anybody was thinking about changing anything?" asked Noah.

"I see," said David. "So what you're telling me is that people do not necessarily fear change, *per se*, but fear the way it is introduced. That makes sense. So how does this relate to my circumstances?"

"I don't believe that you explained to your team that a changing environment is imminent. That might help smooth things over when the change does occur," noted Noah.

"Good idea. I will meet with them and explain the reason for the change," said David. Then he crossed his arms. "But then what?"

"Ask them how they can best support the change. As a team, mind you."

"Solicit their input on how best to implement the change? But how?" asked David. He shook his head from side to side.

"By getting the team to participate in the decision-making process. Then they become owners in the process itself because they have an opportunity to take an active role in the change process."

"Then what?"

"Relax," responded Noah.

"Be patient? That's the key? That's one of the first things you've taught me all along. People need time to adapt to change." David smiled.

"Remember to keep your door and ears open to all comments and suggestions."

"You bet I'll keep communications open. Up and down my chain of command. I want to make sure that I receive feedback from everyone, whether it's good or bad," said David.

"I'm proud of you, sonny."

"You really mean it, Noah? You're really proud of me?"

"You've matured rapidly. Hold your meeting, visualize the concept, and effectuate the change."

"OK, I'll meet with everyone right away. But I still have a remaining question."

"Oh?" asked Noah.

"How do I go about replanning? I mean, actually go about doing it?"

"See you tomorrow," said Noah. He rose from the bench. "Don't follow me or I'll never see you again."

"Right. Tomorrow. Same time. Same place. Take care," said David as he watched the old man stroll away. Patience, he thought. That's just what I need, even when dealing with Noah.

20

Can you turn project lemons into lemonade?

◆

David sat at the head of the conference table. His three leads were staring right at him. He sensed that this wasn't going to be an easy meeting. "Good morning, everyone."

"What's the purpose of this meeting? I didn't get an agenda." asked Ted. "I read through the project manual and it said that all meetings were to have agendas."

"I'm getting to that, Ted, in just a minute." David couldn't help resist the temptation to raise his voice.

"Well, the more time we spend in meetings the less time we have to get the job done." Ted picked up his pad of paper and then tossed it back onto the table.

"Ted, back off," warned Sally. "He has something to say, so let him say it."

"Yes, ma'am," said Ted.

"Thank you, Sally," said David. He felt the flow of blood in his head subside. "This meeting is informal, but highly critical. Folks, we all work for a private concern. It's not like working for a public corporation or a government institution. For that reason, we have to deal with conditions that sometimes seem arbitrary, even capricious."

"What he's saying is BOHICA," said Ted.

"BOHICA? What does that mean?" asked Frank.

"Thanks for your support, Ted. It's an acronym, meaning 'bend over here it comes again,' " said David, shaking his head.

Ted let loose a loud laugh. "I can feel it coming all right."

David tried to pretend Ted didn't exist. "The Yuggenheim family has decided to sell the zoo for a much greater price than anticipated."

"Sounds good for them," said Sally sarcastically.

"Maybe even us. They might keep us on their payroll with another of their companies," added Frank.

David lifted his index finger and tapped it on the wall. "There's only one catch."

"BOHICA!" shouted Ted.

Ignoring him, David continued, "They want to move up the project end date by two months."

"And?" asked Sally.

"With half our current staff and a reduced budget after the reduction in staff," added David.

"How much reduced?" asked Frank.

David felt his Adam's apple sink deeper into his throat. "Ten per cent."

Ted spoke as he pointed his finger directly at David. "Well, I thought it was something serious. I just didn't realize how much so. So how are you going to accomplish this?"

"Why don't you eliminate Ted's job first?" asked Sally.

"What?" asked Ted. "I'll ignore that remark!"

"Yes, how are you going to do this?" asked Frank.

"It's not how *I* am going to do this. It's how *we* are going to do this. This is a team effort. So, team, we need to do some serious replanning," said David.

"I don't get paid to make those kinds of decisions. That's your job. You're the project manager," said Ted, shaking his head.

"Look, Ted, I'm looking for positive input. If you don't have anything constructive to contribute, then please be quiet. You have a wealth of knowledge and experience you could share and your cooperation would be greatly appreciated," said David.

"I say take him off the payroll," said Sally.

"Yeah. He's a lousy poker player anyway," said Frank.

"You've got a lot of nerve, Sally," said Ted. "And so do you, Frank."

"All right, let's cut the bickering," ordered David. "We're professionals here, and that's what I expect from you. So shape up. Part of my task is to prepare a new set of plans for the project. But I can't do that without your help. Can I count on each one of you? Sally?"

"You bet," said Sally.

David turned to Frank. "And?"

"Always," said Frank.

"Ted?" asked David.

A long silence ensued. Then Ted spoke. "Yeah, sure, anytime."

"Great," said David. He forced a confident smile. "Then, let's plan our first replanning session for tomorrow afternoon at one. Here. I'll send out an agenda this afternoon. Sound good? Excellent. In the meantime, I'll meet with each one of you separately. See you all later. Oh, I want to emphasize that my door is open to everyone. And that includes the people supporting you on the project."

"I'd like to meet with the Yuggenheims and tell them what I think. I might even tell them where to put their zoo," said Ted.

"I understand your feelings, Ted," said David. "I'm sure all of us feel the same way to a degree. But we can't allow our resentment to get in the way of achieving our goal. At least we have the opportunity to adapt to the change. To do some effective replanning. Until then, keep your chins up."

As he left the conference, only thoughts of Noah filled his mind.

21

Replanning is not an act of indecisiveness but a calculated move to improve project performance

◆

David and Noah strolled around the open grounds of the zoo. In the centre was a statue of the members of the Yuggenheim family. Strange, even that statue's future looks dismal, he thought.

"Noah, I just don't know," he said with his hands clasped behind his back.

"You just don't know what?" asked Noah, seeming more preoccupied with his pipe than with David.

"What to do next. I've met with my leads and told them about the change, just like you suggested," said David. He took a deep sigh. "I'm also going to get their participation in the replanning effort."

"What seems to be the problem?"

"What's the problem? I'll tell you what's the problem. I have to do some serious replanning in a short period of time."

"You're not the first one. And speaking of first ones, what's the first thing you plan to do?"

"The first thing I need to do . . . let's see . . . Well, I'm going to meet with my first team member in an hour to begin replanning. The only problem is I don't know where to start."

"You start at the beginning. And you are at the beginning. You can't replan without rethinking," said Noah and took a puff from his pipe. "You need to rethink. What do you think needs to be changed?"

"I need to know what needs revising. I could revise the statement of understanding right away."

"Whereabouts?"

"The schedule. Because the project end date has changed. The goal and objectives, however, remain the same."

"What about the tasks?"

"Good point," said David. "If the tasks have to change, I'll need to revise the work breakdown structure. We may be able to remove some tasks and subtasks. That would change other things, too."

"Like what?"

"Like back to the schedule again. Some activities probably won't be in it. We may even have to add other activities. Wow, it's all starting to fall together," said David.

"You mean 'piece together' as opposed to 'fall apart'. Right?"

David felt a rush of adrenalin. "Right! That means we may have to change our time estimates for completing certain activities. We'll probably have to shorten some estimates and lengthen others. That could also mean another change."

"Oh?"

"Yes. Change the logic of the network diagram. The precedence. You know, what comes first, what comes second, and so on. What do you think?"

"I think you're on to something."

"On to a lot of work, if you ask me. Now other things are racing through my mind. I'll need to change the responsibility matrix. I'll need to redo the resource levelling," continued David.

"Why the resource levelling?"

"To see who is most impacted by the changes. Then I can reassign people and change the schedule to accommodate the workload."

"After you change the tasks and schedule, won't the workload shift around?"

"You're right," said David, nodding his head in agreement. "I'll publish the responsibility matrix after doing the resource levelling. Thanks for that insight. Tell me, when you were building the Ark, did God change requirements on you?"

"The world's a changing place. I acted just like you."

"You responded in the same way? How did you manage to redo everything?"

Noah removed his pipe and spoke. "One of man's most valued traits is being adaptable. I was not a shipbuilder by trade. And neither was my staff. I either had to adapt or face the consequences. And the consequences were a little more far reaching than losing my job. Death was imminent. I would be standing on the inside, not the outside of death's door. Sink or swim with nothing in between was my choice. And I chose the latter. Also, I lacked the tools that are available to you today. I had no fancy schmancy gadgetry or measuring devices. In fact, I didn't even have a pick-up truck. I wish I could have had some tools like . . ."

"Tools? Is there something I have now that will help me replan?" questioned David. "Wait a second. Or should I say a microsecond? The microcomputer. After entering the changes, it will produce new resource histograms and a new schedule for me. Then, I can fine-tune everything. So what's next?"

"I give up. You tell me."

"All right. I'll figure it out for myself. Let's see . . . I know I need to determine all the resources required to do the replanning. I've identified the microcomputer. I'll need a room. The conference room will serve that purpose. I'll need people. I'll involve all the leads. Some time, naturally. I think that'll do it," said David. He hastened his pace.

"Are you sure there's nothing you're forgetting?"

"More? Oh, I did forget something. I'll hold a group session after I get everyone's input in order to gain consensus."

"Pretty easy, huh? Once you have figured everything out."

"It all sounds simple enough. But I can tell it won't be easy," said David. "How about a recap?"

"Recap? OK. First, I need to determine what needs to be changed, such as the work breakdown structure. I can do that by meeting individually with my leads. Which ties in with the next point of determining who to meet with."

"And then?"

David took a deep breath and spoke. "Then comes identifying the resources to conduct the replanning effort. That can happen at the same time as determining what needs to be changed and determining who to include in the replanning effort."

"Continue."

"I'll need to incorporate the revisions and hold a meeting with everyone together to resolve differences. Then, I'll finalize any last minute revisions. And distribute copies to everybody. Brilliant, if I may say so myself," said David.

"Good work, but why did you call me? You figured this stuff out yourself."

"You really mean that? You know, I knew how to do this already. But without you, I'd never be able to realize that," said David.

"Is that so?" Noah put his pipe back in his mouth.

"Well, I've got to meet with Ted in about 15 minutes. Thanks for everything, Noah. Thanks," said David. He walked away forgetting that this time he was leaving Noah behind.

22

Listen, not hear

◆

After an exchange of pleasantries, David sat at a table in a far corner of Ted's office. He noticed right away that Ted came and sat opposite him. "Ted, we've got a lot of replanning to do. I . . ."

"Great, more paperwork." Ted crossed his arms.

"Oh?" asked David. "You don't think this is necessary?"

Ted pointed a finger at David. "Look, nothing against you personally, but I've worked on about a dozen projects since I've been with the zoo and we never needed to do all this. All the projects were completed. And I was the project manager for them."

"I see," said David. He fought to restrain himself from getting angry. "Well, if I recall, none finished on time and within budget. And we had three lawsuits, two of which we lost, as a result of the way those projects were handled. Remember the project where the rhino sneaked out of the zoo and was found in the parking area of the shopping centre located three blocks from the zoo? I'm not pointing a finger, Ted. I just want to learn from what we've done before and not repeat the same mistakes."

"Look, we don't have time to discuss past projects. Let's work on this one, OK? We've got a lot of work to do. This administrivia just gets on my nerves." Ted fell back in his chair.

"You liked the earlier plans, didn't you? You said so yourself. And you even signed them." Checkmate, thought David.

"Yeah, yeah, yeah. What do we do first?"

"First, we go over . . ." David showed him the work breakdown structure to see if anything needed alteration. Then he reviewed estimates, followed by the schedule. Finally came the responsibility matrix. "Well, that just about does it. See, that didn't take too long. Only two and half hours."

"It did dispel some of my anxiety about those changes. I feel more comfortable now," admitted Ted. But he still did not smile. "I have an idea who I can release from the project. What's next?"

"I have to meet with Sally and Frank to get their input to make the revisions accordingly, print out new charts and diagrams, even a set of histograms. Then I'll hold a group meeting to resolve any differences. And finally make those changes and that'll do it."

"Makes sense. Will we each get a copy of the revisions?"

"You bet. All we'll need to do is to insert them into the project manual."

"I guess I was worrying needlessly about the changes. I just felt that all sense of reality was ignored. And the pressure of losing my job was too much to handle. But these new plans make me, and most likely the others, feel more confident," said Ted.

"Good," said David as he extended his hand. "The group meeting will be at 11am this Wednesday, adjacent to my conference room. See you then." He felt the tight grip of Ted's hand and then walked out of the office, smiling.

23

Every decision has an impact: positive, negative, or both

◆

Sitting in front of his microcomputer David entered the changes into the project management database and generated reports. He practically leaned into the monitor in anticipation of the results.

Let's see, he thought. I've entered changes to the estimates and changed the logic of the schedule. I now have some start-to-start relationships rather than just finish-to-start. I've re-assigned people to activities as requested. Now, let's run the resource histograms for each team member. Let's give Ted a shot. Hmmm . . . Oh my God! I've got him working 34 hours per day sometimes at three week stretches! What about Sally? Help, she'll be eaten alive, too. Let's see what the budget calls for. Just as I thought: it's higher because of the overtime paid. Well, back to the drawing board. But first, I'm calling Noah for some insight.

He grabbed the receiver from the phone on his desk and called Freephone—NOAH. He heard a click and didn't wait for Noah to speak.

"Noah, it's me," said David.

"Hello me. What's new at the zoo?"

"Am I the only person who calls you?" asked David. "You always seem to guess correctly."

Noah chuckled. "What do you need?"

"Here's what I've done . . ." said David.

"Let me guess. You made changes to your project and entered them on your microcomputer. Am I close?"

"That's exactly what I did," said David, surprised by Noah's insight. "But the new histogram's peaks are higher and the estimated budget is actually higher as a result of the estimated overtime to be paid. I can't compress the schedule any further."

"What about the alternatives?"

"What alternatives?"

"Alternatives to reduce your increased budget and labour. Can you come up with any?"

David paused to think. Then he spoke. "I could hire contract work which might be cheaper than using my own people. But isn't there a problem using contract work?"

"Yes. Sometimes you get what you pay for. And sometimes you get less than what you pay for. On the other hand, sometimes you get more than you care to know. And sometimes, you get what you want," said Noah. "Clear?"

"Yes, I think so. Anyway, I could also streamline operations. Reduce the number of approvals and forms to complete. But that, too, poses some problems," said David.

"You could lose something in the translation. And be too far gone before you realize it. Recovery is difficult."

"I could cancel vacations and any training opportunities," added David. "Fortunately, I have no training planned, but who knows what someone might need in the future?"

"Taking away people's vacation time is a sore point. Some folks have saved up and planned all year to go to some exotic hide-away. And maybe even persuaded grandma to take care of the kids for a week or two. Training is interesting; sometimes, two or three days' worth of training saves two or three weeks of trying to figure it out for yourself," said Noah.

"You're right, Noah," agreed David. "Those are problems associated with cutting back training and vacations. I could have everyone use cheaper supplies and materials and services — although I can definitely see problems with taking that action, too."

"You might be able to cut back here. But how much depends on what you can do with what you have. And how the results are affected."

"And those are just a few ramifications, Noah. Even lowering the quality of output can reduce budget and help meet the schedule. But that can prove difficult, too."

"It's like the astronauts," said Noah, followed by a slight cough. "Would you go to the moon in a spaceship that was built by the lowest bidder? Think about it. Another approach is shift work."

"Exactly," concurred David. "I could use shift work. That will lower some of the labour costs. For tasks requiring two people or more, I could have one work the first eight hours and the other work the second eight hours."

"Will they make notes for each other?" asked Noah. "I hope so, because no person-to-person meeting will be possible."

"You're right. I can hear and see the problems already. I have two other options, though."

"Speak up."

And David did. "I can concentrate on the critical activities and forget the noncritical ones temporarily until they become critical. Or, I can rework the schedule again and cut work on some activities and allow more work on the critical ones."

"You do have another option," noted Noah. "And that's the *status quo*. That means leaving things the way they are. Everything has some minimum time to complete. Or else it fails. Your project included. Work out the impacts of the

Yuggenheim edict, and show your boss its — excuse the term — unreasonableness. Maybe the Yuggenheims aren't aware of the implications. So you should request them to reconsider. First off, however, you need to make all the changes to the best of your and your team's ability, and compare that with the *status quo*."

"I think I'll work on the project plans a little more, only this time getting the leads' input and then present the plan to the Yuggenheims. They, too, will have to face reality! One more question for you, Noah."

"Go."

"Would you like to attend the group session with my leads?" asked David. "That way you can tell me how I'm managing them."

"What's that have to do with the third secret? And, don't forget you're only three out of four."

"What do you mean I'm only three out of four?" asked David. "Yes, I'm still on the third secret, not the fourth one. But, I don't even know what the third secret is."

"Sure you do."

"I do? What? Tell me."

"Gotta go. 'Bye. I have faith in you. You'll figure it out."

David heard the all too familiar click. "I just wish there was some way I could control him. Wait a minute. That is the third secret! Control! I must control the project. I've been learning how to control a project. Noah, you're brilliant. Even when you're not on the phone," he said as he replaced the receiver.

24

Do your meetings encourage brainstorming sessions or thunder showers?

◆

The conference room was now a familiar place. David and his leads sat around the large table. Printouts were attached to the walls with tape. In front of each person was a stack of paper.

David spoke. "What you have in front of you is what is posted on the walls, a copy of the project plans that have been revised to reflect the latest requirements established by the Yuggenheim family. The changes in the work breakdown structure, the estimates, the network and its logic, and the responsibility matrix incorporate the changes that you suggested when I held independent conversations with each of you. Notice that I had to incorporate some changes to eliminate unrealistic workloads that were reflected in the resource histograms. The histograms start on page . . ."

Ted slapped his hand on the table. "Eliminate unrealistic workloads! I want to see my histogram and the ones generated for each of my people working on the project. What page are they on?"

"All right. Turn to page seven. There's your group's histogram, Ted. What do you think?" asked David.

"I think . . . it looks good," said Ted. He fell back in his chair.

"I don't believe it! Ted likes something," said Sally.

"Now let's look at Sally's histogram and the ones for her people," suggested David. He turned towards Sally. "Yours is on page 16."

"I'll say it again. I don't believe it. I'm working 18 hours a day for 13 straight days! I can't handle that type of workload. I don't even think a super-hero can handle that much," she said.

"Glad you brought that up. You'll notice that most of your activities are not on the critical path and have plenty of float," said David.

"So?" she asked.

"That means that even though you have a large number of peaks in the histogram, you can let some of the activities causing those peaks slide because they're not on the critical path. Therefore you don't have to start working on them on the day indicated. In reality, the peaks in your histogram will probably not occur. So, it looks like you're OK, too," said David. He made it a point to smile at her.

"I was hoping you'd work her to the bone. Or at least until she dropped dead. It couldn't happen to a more deserving woman," sneered Ted.

"You're a jerk, Ted. While Ted was groaning on, I thumbed through the other histograms. They all look great. Nice job," she said.

"Even for me and my people?" asked Frank.

"Frank, you're on page 23 and your people's follow thereafter. Seems your histograms are completely level. It looks about as favourable as you can get. As everyone can see, the plans reveal that we can, in fact, deliver our project with less money and less time than originally thought. That is, if nothing goes wrong," said David. He crossed his fingers to symbolize what he meant.

"If something does go wrong, what can we do? How will we get back on track?" asked Sally.

"Contingency planning," noted David. "We're going to develop contingency plans right now for every conceivable problem that could arise. Let's brainstorm by free-thinking. Let's anticipate a problem and develop what is known as a 'workaround' to overcome the problem."

Everyone began brainstorming the possible negative happenings that could occur on the project. They then prioritized each occurrence as high, medium, or low, and identified possible workarounds.

"This list looks good," said David as he admired it. "I'll get it typed up and Frank, you place it in the project manual along with the other updated documentation that was generated. It will serve as good reference material."

"So what's next?" asked Ted.

"Yes, what happens now?" asked Sally.

"Keep me tuned in," requested Frank.

"The next step is to give a presentation to Craig Yuggenheim. He's the family member who's the point of contact for this project," said David.

"I still don't like this whole project. Dismantle the zoo." Ted sneered. "You can tell old Craig Yuggenheim what I think of him, his family, and this whole project."

"Come on, Ted. Let's not get abrasive," said David.

"Ted's not abrasive; he just wears sandpaper for underwear," said Sally with a laugh. Frank started to laugh, too.

"Oh, yeah. Well, you wear a 24-hour bra. We work eight hours a day, so you figure that you only have to wash it every fourth day," said Ted.

"OK, enough," ordered David. "Let's focus on what needs to be done for the welfare of the animals. Before we end this meeting, I would like everyone's initials on the work breakdown structure and the network diagram."

"Why?" asked Frank.

Ted chuckled loudly. "He wants to take the fame but spread the blame."

"Ted, cool your smart remarks," warned David. "I just want to show my boss that everyone here has provided input to the new set of schedules and breed commitment on our part to meet those schedules."

"I assume you'll sign it too?" asked Ted.

"If you look in the signature block, you'll notice that I've already signed it." David looked at his female lead. "Sally?"

"My pleasure," said Sally.

"Frank?" asked David.

"You bet," said Frank.

"Ted?" asked David.

"I'm not signing anything. No way," said Ted, backing away from the table while in his chair. "I didn't agree to those ridiculous requirements by the Yuggenheims. They must have been smoking something pretty strong. I'll work to it to the best of my ability, but I won't sign. And that's that."

"Stubborn cuss, aren't you?" asked Sally.

"OK, that's his choice, folks," said David. "But tell us, Ted, what would get you to sign the documents?" asked David.

"Ahhh . . . well . . ." said Ted.

"You did get the opportunity to provide input, didn't you?" asked David.

"Yeah, sure, but . . . all right, I'll sign the damn paperwork," said Ted. He dragged himself closer to the table, yanked his pen from his shirt pocket, and signed the document. "There, you happy now?"

"Great," said David. "Now I'm ready to deal with my boss and Craig Yuggenheim. So let's get on with the show. Also note that the budget report reflects a decline in the requested monies to be spent on our project. So, just keep in mind that we're also working with fewer shekels, er, dollars. See you all at our status review meeting in four days. Keep up the good work." He rose from the table and left the room. Thank God it's over, he thought. At least for the moment.

25

Vertical communication does not mean getting the shaft

◆

In front of a large oak desk, decorated with gold and brass trinkets, sat David and Harrison. Behind the desk and in a black leather swivel chair sat Craig Yuggenheim.

"Mr. Yuggenheim . . ." said David.

"Young man, before you begin, I just want to say that I am very impressed with the initial set of plans that you put together. They were quite professional," said Yuggenheim as he blew his nose in a grey silk handkerchief with his initials embroidered on it. He wore a dark purple cravat that edged from his light blue shirt. Although he wore slacks, the casual appearance looked deceiving. David knew that the slacks alone cost more than his own entire outfit, shoes included.

"Thank you, sir," said David.

"You bet they were," said Harrison. He then cleared his throat. "I was quite pleased, too."

"Thanks," said David. "As you both know, some changes were requested that forced us to reconsider and revise our plans."

"That's correct. Go on," said the wealthy businessman.

David obeyed. "These new conditions required some substantial replanning. That meant revisions to the statement of understanding. You have a revised copy in front of you. Please take a few moments to read what it says."

Yuggenheim looked at the paper.

"Yes, that's right. Go on, young man."

"Mr. Yuggenheim, now look at the work breakdown structure," said David. "I've added some tasks and subtasks and deleted others."

"Looks good." Yuggenheim turned to Harrison. "Doesn't it?"

"Yes, sir. Best work breakdown structure I've ever seen," said Harrison.

David continued. "I've put together, based on the highest level items of the work breakdown structure, a bar chart. Each bar represents the flow time for a phase of the project. It represents the first tier of the work breakdown structure."

Yuggenheim shifted his weight in the chair. "What about the tasks that are delivered in each phase — where are they listed? They're not on this chart. How can you maintain control of our project when you don't know what more specific tasks . . ."

"Mr. Yuggenheim, turn to the next page. On it you will see the task breakdown or second tier of the work breakdown structure. It identifies, by task and by phase, the work that needs to be performed. And if you want even more detail, the next page shows the subtask breakdown or third tier of the work breakdown structure," said David.

Yuggenheim turned the pages. "Looks very thorough. I'll review it in detail later. Nice work, gentlemen."

"Thanks. The first tier bar chart is best used for management reporting. That's because most managers are not interested in the details. At least not upfront." David smiled. "I included the other tier charts as backup information for you."

"He learned that from me, sir," said Harrison.

"Tell me, were you able to reduce your project team in order to meet the budgetary requests I submitted?" asked Yuggenheim.

"Yes he did, sir," said Harrison.

"The question was directed to your protégé," said Yuggenheim.

David did not want to be in an adversarial position with Harrison. "My boss is right. I was able to do that. If you turn to the budget report, you'll see that the estimate for completing the project is less than half what was originally estimated."

"And the project end date?" asked Yuggenheim.

"We can meet that, too," said David.

"Show him the histograms that we generated," said Harrison.

"If you turn to the histograms in your document you'll see that virtually all the people remaining are working a full eight to ten-hour day from the beginning of the project to its completion," said David. "There's no time for relaxation, even training."

"It certainly looks packed, that's for sure," observed Yuggenheim. "I was going to ask if you could cut the work force even more and move the schedule date forward another month but from the look of these documents that would prove near impossible. You did some really fine planning here, young man. Where did you learn to do all this?"

"From someone whom I believe is very wise and knowledgeable," said David.

"Why thank you," said Harrison.

"Sure," said David just to avoid a showdown later. "I also learned it from someone from the past. Someone who has used these techniques in the real world on a grand scale."

"Well, whenever you see him again, tell him there's always room for him in one of my companies," said Yuggenheim.

David nodded his head and said, "I'll do that, sir."

"I notice that the summary cost and schedule reports and the bar charts were printed out by some kind of computer," said Yuggenheim as he thumbed through the pages.

"We used a microcomputer with project management software on it," said Harrison.

"He's correct. The package took some time and effort to learn, but it enabled me . . . I mean us . . . to develop the plans that meet your constraints," added David.

Yuggenheim looked at his watch. "Well, I have another meeting coming up. I just want to add that you both did a great job. I feel very confident now that we'll meet the requirements agreed to in the contract. Good work gentlemen. One of these days I'll be out at the zoo to see how things are going." He then smiled and said, "Unannounced."

"I'll be glad to see you, sir," said Harrison.

"So will I," said David, extending his hand. But he didn't get to shake hands with Craig Yuggenheim; Harrison had pushed him aside.

26

A visibility wall is not a wailing wall

◆

David met with Noah at a bench in the area of the zoo called the Family Farm, where children could pet animals. He sat next to his old friend. They watched people leave the parking lot on the other side of the fence.

"Noah, I don't know how I can thank you." David shook Noah's hand. "In the short time that I've known you, I've gained so much knowledge about project management. Why, I've learned stuff that other men twice my age never knew. And some probably never will. I can't thank you enough."

Noah pushed his fisherman's cap back on his head, pointed his finger in the air, and said, "You're not done yet."

"What?" asked David. "There's more?"

"Learning never stops. And for now, you know three secrets of project management."

"I remember them. Planning, organizing, and controlling."

"Very good." Noah lit his porcelain pipe and let out a huge cloud of purple smoke.

"I'm glad you're satisfied. So what's the fourth secret?" asked David. He couldn't resist the temptation to ask even though he knew Noah wouldn't give it.

"You're not ready for it yet."

"What do you mean I'm not ready yet? I've learned quickly so far."

"You aren't fully saturated with the third secret."

"You say that there's still more to controlling?" asked David. "Look, you'd better tell me what it is. And quickly. Because Craig Yuggenheim is going to visit the zoo and see how the project is proceeding."

"Do you have a visibility wall for him to see how the project is proceeding?"

"What do you mean, do I have a visibility wall? Sure I do. In my office."

"David, your office is your living environment. Not a visibility wall. The visibility wall is usually in a war room."

"You mean like something at an army headquarters?"

"Or like at a children's daycare centre. The war room allows you and your team to create, brainstorm, and beat on each other, in a constructive manner. And the visibility wall displays your efforts," said Noah.

"What does this visibility wall look like?"

"The wall board material should accommodate pushpins," said Noah. "Masking tape is out since it ruins the finish of the wall. But, if you really have money to spend, the wall will be magnetic."

"Magnetic?"

"So that you can attach your charts, reports, and other paperwork using magnets instead of pushpins. It's a great idea, but it is costly."

"Wow, that sounds impressive. The type of display depends on the magnitude of the project. I bet that for a small project you can use just a wall in an office," said David. "Not a bad idea but what purposes does it serve?"

"It lets you see what you're doing and gives you a grasp of not only the details, but the big picture, too," continued Noah. "And it's there right in front of you. All of it. So you can gain perspective of what's going on. And what's not. Also, it provides the entire team with the same opportunity. All at the same time. So there's no confusion even over who is looking at what. Everybody's looking at the same thing at the same time." He took a few puffs on his pipe. He then started blowing smoke rings.

"Did you have one on the Ark?" asked David.

"No way I could have done without it."

"You did?" asked David. "What did it look like?"

Noah blew one big ring and then rested his pipe in his hand. "Mine was sectioned off. One section of the wall was dedicated to the statement of understanding, another was for the work breakdown structure, a third was for high level schedules, a fourth was for budgets, a fifth was for contract labour. And, of course, there was one gigantic section dedicated to the actual construction and responsibilites.

"Oh, I almost forgot a very important section," continued Noah. "The organizational chart, or to put it in your terms 'who's who in the zoo'. The principles remain the same; however, technology improved the formatting, reporting, and display media."

"Should I use a wall in my office?"

"Those walls are not large enough to display your project's information. And your walls are already covered with your work. Besides, there might be enough room for the team to sit, but it's not neutral territory."

"I think you're right. I could use a conference room. And hold my meetings in there, too. Even though I've declared my office as being open to everyone, it's not a place where people feel they can freely come and go. In a conference room they would be able to see the wall at their convenience. Brilliant, Noah. This room will knock Craig Yuggenheim's socks off! Guaranteed," said David.

"I'm glad you approve."

"One more question, Noah."

"Go ahead."

"Do you have some time so I can show you around the offices?"

"Not a lot. Why?"

"I'd like you to help me figure out where's the best place to put the visibility wall in the conference room," said David.

"On any of the four walls, for starters." Noah put his pipe back in his mouth.

"Seriously, Noah. I'd also like you to meet some of the team members and observe how things are going."

"Can't say that I have the time."

"Please, Noah. Just this once. I'll buy you dinner. Anything you want. Please."

"All right, but just this once, mind you. Let's go." Noah rose to his feet and headed towards the exit a short distance away.

"Now? You mean right now?" asked David. He jumped to his feet and followed the old man.

Noah nodded his head.

"OK, let's hop in my car and off we go," said David. They approached a metallic blue sportscar.

"I'd prefer to *step* into your car."

"Have it your own way," said David as he opened the door of the passenger side of his car. "Have it your own way."

Noah stepped into the vehicle.

Then David leaped over the door of the driver's side and fell into the seat. "Let's go," he said as he turned the ignition key, revved the engine, and put the car in gear.

27

Not all walls block communication

◆

They walked into the office. The room was dark until David reached for the light switch. "Well, what do think of my digs?"

"Pleasant surroundings." Noah created a cloud of purple smoke from his pipe. "Don't mind the smoke?"

"No. It smells a lot better than my boss's cigar. Have a seat here," said David, pointing to a chair next to his desk.

Noah tossed his fisherman's cap onto the desk. Then he repositioned the chair so that it didn't face the desk, picked up the telephone, and made a call. All David heard was Noah saying, "I'll be a bit late. Start without me." He then hung up the receiver.

"You act as though you've moved in," noted David. "If you want a job, Craig Yuggenheim said you could have one anytime in one of his companies. Who was that you were talking to? I hope I'm not delaying you."

"Enough already. Let's get on track."

"Right, back to business. Now, do you think the wall over there would make a good visibility wall?" asked David.

"We're in your office, not a meeting room. We talked about a dedicated space."

"So we did — I agreed that the conference room would make a good meeting area. And the visibility wall would be in it. All right, I'll concede that." David then asked, "What would you put on the wall?"

Noah looked around the room as he stroked his beard, adjusted his hat, and puffed on his pipe. "Paper. Wall paper."

"Right. Let me figure it out."

"Take it in small chunks. Start with the first thing you'd want to see."

"What would be the first thing I'd put on the wall? I know, Noah. A title."

"Good. That would tell everyone what project the wall's about."

"And, how about a copy of the statement of understanding? That way everyone can see what the project is to accomplish."

"Very good, David. What else?"

"I'd then display the work breakdown structure. At least a high level version of it. That way everyone sees what phase we are in and what's left to do."

"I'd go down to the lowest level version. That way each team member can see the tasks which they and the others have to perform," said Noah.

David agreed. "You're right. I'll also display a schedule. Probably a picture of the network diagram, too, and maybe even a bar chart."

"Personally, I'd go beyond that. Organizationally everyone should know who's who in the zoo," said Noah.

"The organization chart would be a good addition to the wall. That shows the reporting structure for the project."

"What about a facilities layout?" asked Noah.

"A map of the zoo?" asked David. "I'll buy that. It will make discussions concerning the zoo easier to comprehend, especially when we talk about any particular section or area."

"You're starting to realize that you are the owner of the wall. And as the owner, you can do as you please," said Noah.

"You're right. The wall can have almost anything on it. You know, I might even want to display a copy of the most recent reports."

"Reports about what?"

David shrugged, thinking the answer was self-evident. "Reports concerning budget, schedule, and quality. That's what I'd show. I'll tell you, Noah, having a visibility wall will increase my control over the project. I'll be able to keep everyone informed and keep everyone focused on the project, especially during meetings. You've really taught me a lot about the third secret, controlling. I presume that the fourth secret will prove as enlightening as the other three?"

"You presume correctly. And the fourth secret runs in parallel with the other three."

"The fourth secret occurs during planning, organizing, and controlling a project? What could that be?" asked David.

"Or, do you mean 'How could that be?'"

David pointed his finger at Noah and said, "I know you want me to derive what the fourth secret is myself. So it occurs during planning, organizing, and controlling? All right. But before we get to it, I'd like to introduce you to my leads." David looked at his watch. "I've got a status review meeting in just 20 minutes. I'd like you to attend."

"Why?" Noah pounded his pipe on the edge of David's desk.

"Why? Why?" asked David. "I value your insights. That's why."

"OK," said Noah as he emptied the remnants of tobacco from his pipe onto a blank sheet of paper on David's desk.

"Thanks for not pouring that stuff into my coffee cup. Or the waste basket. Here's a magazine to read while I prepare for the meeting," said David, a bit disgruntled, as he tossed a magazine to his ancient friend.

Noah leafed through the pages. "Here's a good article. 'How Your Company Can Save Money by Outsourcing.' "

"What's outsourcing?" asked David.

"Hiring outside help because you don't have either the time, knowledge, or resources to accomplish the task."

"Oh," said David, noticing the smile that just returned to Noah's face while browsing through the rest of the magazine and puffing steadily on his pipe.

28

You can't manage a project if you can't manage yourself

◆

The team leads huddled around the table eyeing one another. David stood between two overhead projectors at the far end of the table. He looked about, confused, wondering what happened to Noah. "Wait a minute folks. Before we get started, I have to . . ."

He rushed to the entrance of the conference room, stuck his head in the hallway and looked around. But his friend was nowhere.

"Are we ready to get started? I don't have all day," shouted Ted.

"Yes, let's get on with business," agreed Sally.

"Yeah. Move it," concurred Frank.

"All right, hold still," said David. He pulled his body back into the conference room. "I want to mention a few things before we start our status meeting."

"Let's just collect status. That's why we're here," said Ted.

"Look, Ted, I'm running the show, not you," snapped David.

"You tell him, David," encouraged Sally.

"The issue is between me and him, not you babe," said Ted.

"I'm not your babe," she said.

David tried to ignore the negative remarks. "I had my meeting with Craig Yuggenheim. He was impressed with what we have done. He wants me to extend his appreciation to all of you."

"How benevolent of him. It's because of him and the rest of his family that we're in this boat," said Ted. "Greedy bastards."

Frank joined in. "Life's a bitch."

"Don't use that word around me, Frank. That's a sexist remark," Sally said.

"Sorry, but so is being called a babe. Why don't you chide Ted?" Frank's voice quivered.

"Listen, everyone! We're here to collect status. Ted, let's go over your tasks in the schedule first," said David.

Ted gave status on all his activities in the schedule.

Then David asked about one of Ted's tasks. "Why did you make a decision like that? I don't understand how anyone with your experience could perform that task that way."

"Hey, pal, if you think you can do a better job, then do it yourself," replied Ted, slamming his fist on the table. "I don't have to take that from you or anybody. Besides, if you knew why I did what I did, you wouldn't jump to conclusions."

"OK, Sally, your turn," said David. He just wished Ted would disappear. He then covered her schedule items.

"Everything appears OK," observed David. "You're right on schedule. Except for one task. Very good . . . wait a second. That task is sliding. And it feeds directly to the one that Ted handled in a strange way."

"I told you I had a reason for what I did. Otherwise, I'd be really behind schedule. I'll have to do some rework because of her. But at least I got something done," interjected Ted.

David ignored the remark. "I notice, too, that the tasks you completed, Sally, are the noncritical ones. Why's that?"

"I never liked you and now I know the reason," said Sally, pointing at Ted. She turned towards David and said, "All right, I'll get the task done. I promise."

"Make sure it's done right, too. I don't have time for your wishy-washy attitude," said Ted.

"OK. Frank, it's your turn," said David.

"I'm happy to say that everything is going fine. No problems. I'm on schedule. I've completed everything that needs to be completed," said Frank.

"Let's discuss each activity, then," said David. He covered each item in the schedule related to Frank.

"Now that we have discussed each item, I can tell you that not all the tasks were started on time or done completely. You were less than candid with me, Frank," said David as he pointed his finger.

"Made a mistake, sir. What I thought and what actually occurred . . . I guess were two different things," confessed Frank.

"Well, enough of the guessing. Try to stay on top of things," said David.

"Yes, sir," said Frank. He mocked a military salute.

"Now that we've had our status review, I'll enter the new information into the computer and get an updated schedule and set of reports. You'll get them tomorrow at the one o'clock meeting. For those of you who have problems meeting the schedule and may have overrun your budget, make sure you correct the situation. OK?" asked David.

Everyone nodded their head in affirmation, except one person. Ted. He just gave an angry stare at Sally.

David noticed the tension but wanted to ignore it. He turned off the overhead projectors and said, "Good. Now let me explain what a visibility wall means to you . . ."

29

Conflict is not bad; only the way it is handled

◆

David stormed into his office. Noah had his feet on the desk and his hands behind his head as he puffed on his pipe and stroked his grey beard.

"Where the hell were you? And get your feet off my desk," screamed David.

Noah dropped his feet from the desk and sat upright. "You sound distressed. Something happen at your meeting?"

"Something happen?" asked David, with his jaw hanging open. "No kidding something happened! I just went through the worst meeting in my life. That's what happened."

"Is that what really happened?"

"Huh? What do you mean, was that what really happened? I just told you it was," snapped David.

"You just told me your feelings. The worst meeting in your life. That's also your subjective outcome. You're not being objective. And I know, because I heard everything," said Noah.

"You heard everything? How?" asked David.

Noah picked up on the Indian greeting and followed through. "Me listen through conference room door opening. That how. Me pretend to be janitor. You no notice me. You unaware of surroundings; concentrate only on your needs, not on what going on around you. Was easy for me. Me leave quickly at meeting's end. You continue on though, about visibility wall."

David couldn't resist releasing a nervous chuckle. Then his face turned serious. "Enough of the Indian dialect. You deserted me."

"You toss words around as if people have no feelings. I'm going." Noah rose from his chair.

"What? Leaving me again?" David changed his tone of voice. "Look, Noah, I'm sorry. Really I am. It's just that I'm so stressed out," said David.

"That's easily understandable." Noah sank into his chair. "Are you ready to tell me what really happened?"

"Yeah," said David, as he, too, sank into a chair next to his desk.

"Go ahead."

"You heard just about everything?"

Noah nodded his head.

"I'm embarrassed," said David.

"You should be embarrassed. Not ashamed, mind you, but embarrassed."

"Yeah, I know I've got real problems on my hands," confessed David. "So, what did I do wrong?"

"I'm glad you realize that you have more than one problem to work on. Let's explore each one individually."

"That sounds like a good game plan. Give me lesson number one."

"Did your meeting have any order or direction? Or did chaos reign supreme?"

"No, I didn't have order or direction in the meeting. Would I be in this mental shape if I had?" asked David. "Long live King Chaos."

"No need for a long chaotic life here. Arise ye o' Attractive Agenda. By having an agenda, everyone will know what topics to discuss at the meeting. And if you indicate the time allotted for each agenda item, your team will get an idea as to how long your meeting is really planned to last," said Noah.

"Then what I needed was an agenda? Why didn't I think about that?" David tapped his forehead. "It is required in the project manual. The meeting probably would have been less strenuous and gone quicker if I operated according to the project manual. Good point. I'll pass it out in advance so that everyone will know what will be covered when and how much time is allocated. Now, what's lesson number two?"

"Why collect status at the review meeting? Why not collect it beforehand?"

"Collect status before the status review meeting? Then why have a status review meeting at all?"

Noah leaned in his chair towards the young executive. "The purpose of the status meeting is to assess how well things are going. That means collecting the data first, and then generating new schedules and reports in order to make the appropriate assessment at the meeting. In reality you only need one meeting, but the way you're working it you need two."

"You're right," agreed David. "I just didn't think about getting status on each activity in the schedule before the meeting and then generating the reports. We then could make an assessment where we are in terms of meeting the cost, schedule, and quality targets for the project." He let loose a sigh and took a deep breath.

"Your face indicates to me that you think we're done. We're not."

"Not through?" David's voice became tense. "I don't understand. Boy, I really blew it. OK, give me the next lesson." He threw his hands up into the air.

"A classic mistake you made was jumping to conclusions before hearing all the facts. That's bad medicine."

"What do mean bad medicine, Noah? I had a reason for what I did. It may not have been right, but . . ."

"But you did it anyway. You didn't stop to think. You didn't stop to mull it over. You just jumped on your bandwagon and came out with both barrels blazing."

"Enough, Noah. Let me get a word in edgeways. I'll tell you why."

"No, sonny," chuckled Noah. "I'll tell you why, why Ted felt the way he did. And how you treated, or shall I say mistreated, him in front of his peers. Let me ask you, how do you think Ted felt in the conversation, being evaluated without having a chance to explain his reason? But much worse, you came across as if you were attacking Ted personally. And my guess is that he felt just like you feel now."

"Yes, I must admit I did get a little judgmental with Ted. Then I did find out that it was Sally who caused the problem, not Ted. Boy, what a mistake. Ted probably wants to put me six feet under," said David.

"Or more. And I bet you were angry with me, too, just now."

David nodded his head. "Yes, I was angry with you. Ted must feel the same way about me. And you're right, I criticized him rather than determining the cause of the problem. And to make matters worse, I did it in front of his peers. Oh, what a screw-up."

"I hope you learned something here."

David coughed and then spoke. "Well, I learned that I will collect information from everyone first and that includes their opinions. Then I should make an evaluative judgment as to the status and not of the person, and then identify the causes of any problems. There's only one thing that confuses me," said David.

"Only one? I'm impressed."

"Why did Frank lie?"

"To disguise the reality of the situation. And to save himself from your wrath." Noah removed his hat and stroked his thinning grey hair.

David shook his head again. "You're right. If I were Frank, I would have lied, too. He feared criticism in front of everyone and saw the way I reacted. Makes sense that he would lie. I'd do the same, come to think of it. No wonder he wanted to meet with me after the meeting and discuss some concerns."

"It's better to surface any concerns or problems in front of the entire group," said Noah. "That way everyone gets a chance to help brainstorm a solution. And everyone can determine what impact the problem and its alternative solutions will have on their areas."

"That's right. There were concerns that should have been discussed with everyone present. Well, thanks for your insights, I'll remember them all. That's a fact." David started to rise.

"The look on your face indicates that you think we're done. My lips to your ears will change that."

"Another lesson? And what's that?" asked David, falling into his chair.

Noah placed his cap on his head and stroked his beard. "Don't tell someone to fix something without being specific. Discuss problems. Identify causes. Suggest alternative solutions. Be specific in your direction."

"I see," agreed David as he had done so many times before. "I did end the status review session telling everyone to fix the problems causing the schedule slide that will show up when I enter the status into the computer later on. That wasn't very smart. How can they fix something when they have no idea what was the cause? And what are the methods of cause detection and prevention?"

"It's analogous to going to the doctor with a pain. The doctor looks at you and tells you to get better. And soon."

"I like that analogy. You're right." Then David asked, "OK, but what can I do to eliminate a schedule slide or budget overrun or poor quality other than do things better?"

"Doing things better implies doing things smarter. But that's for discussion at another time."

"All right. We'll discuss that later. Where are you going?" asked David.

"Home," answered Noah. He rose from his chair and headed towards the exit.

"Home?" asked David. He jumped to his feet. "But I want to show you around the administration building to give you an idea of my working environment."

"Some other time, OK?"

David knew it was a demand rather than a request. "Fine. See you tomorrow after the status meeting. Take care. And thanks again," said David. "Need a ride?"

"No." Noah slammed the door behind him.

What a grouch, thought David. But I don't want him angry at me, too. Now, how do I improve schedule, budget and quality performance?

30

Participative decision-making does not absolve you from responsibility

◆

David looked at his gold watch. It was getting late in the night. A grimace was planted on his face. What the hell, he thought. It's been about a week since we last talked. He reached for the phone and pressed the digital buttons. "Noah? Is that you?"

"What? Who is this? Do you know what time it is?"

David recognized the voice right away. "Sorry. Didn't mean to . . ."

"I hope this is important. I'm trying to . . ."

"The situation looks grim, damn grim, Noah."

"Did you start working on fixing it?"

"Well, I don't know where to start."

"Time. Try time."

"You mean the schedule?" asked David. "But it looks so damn dismal."

"What does your critical path look like?"

David took a deep sigh and said, "The critical path items have all slid. According to the schedule report and the network diagram I just generated on my microcomputer, the estimate-at-completion is two weeks beyond the scheduled project delivery date. The project is just too early in its development to have that kind of slide."

"Money? What about money?"

"The budget? Well, the new estimate at completion for the project is 23 per cent beyond the original estimate. The costs for the critical path tasks really did a job on the budget. It doesn't look good at all," said David.

"What's that noise I hear coming from your side of the phone? It sounds like you're shaking in your boots."

"Listen here, I'm not getting panicky," shot David in a high pitched voice. Then it dropped to a lower tone. "Things just aren't going the way I expected them to."

"It's OK to be nervous," said Noah. "It keeps you thinking. It's also OK to be calm and confident. What about your project's quality?"

"Quality of performance? Boy, can I tell you about quality! I've got calls coming in at just about the speed of light," said David.

"You must be very popular. Who's calling you?"

David sighed. "Contractors, contractors, and more contractors. Contractors are complaining about the lack of cooperation between the project team and themselves. Half of the tasks are being redone."

"What are you doing about it?"

"I don't know. What should I do?"

"How should I know? The contractors are calling you, not me."

"Look, Noah, I called for help. Not for you to tell me to figure it out myself."

"You have the power of authority for your project, David, not me. So use it."

"OK, Noah. I realize that I'm supposed to make decisions on my own."

"I didn't say that. I didn't say that you should make decisions on your own. You said that."

David grew impatient with the conversation. "Wrong again? Does that mean that I shouldn't be making all the decisions myself? I thought you just said that I was the project manager and had the power of authority?"

"You are the project manager," instructed Noah. "And you have the power of authority. But that doesn't mean that you have to make all the decisions alone. Your people, your team, have a need and a want for participative decision-making. They have opinions that are valuable and should be considered before you make the final decision. By leaving them out of the decision-making process, you not only tend to crush their enthusiasm, but you also lose out on listening to their inputs."

"With people like Ted and Sally? They're complainers. They complain all the time. I can see them lynching me by the end of tomorrow's meeting. I'd be a dead duck. I can't do it, Noah."

"Let me put it to you this way, sonny. Your *status quo* ain't so hot now either. It's time for a change, before things really get out of hand."

David didn't expect Noah to be so blunt. "You know, you might be right. If I get their participation on how to resolve some of these difficulties, it might turn out for the better. You're right, I don't have anything to lose."

"The only thing you have to lose is your fear of doing it."

"Good point. Their input makes my job easier and gets them off my back. Maybe even the morale will get better. But can't you give me some ideas on how to fix my schedule, budget, and quality problems? Just some hints," pleaded David.

"Keep thinking, sonny. It'll come to you."

"Noah, to change the subject for a moment. Why don't you tell me the fourth secret?"

"What's to tell? You know it already!"

"You mean that I've been learning it all along?" asked David. "I thought right now I've been learning about controlling."

"You are learning controlling, but you've been learning about the fourth secret all along while planning and organizing, too. Sometimes it's hard to see the forest for the trees," said Noah.

"You're kidding? I don't believe it! But I can't tell what it is," said David.

Noah released a loud yawn. "I'll give you a clue, David. It's not as tangible as the other three secrets, but without it the project would fail. A first class fail, mind you. And by the way, David, you'll have to use the fourth secret at tomorrow's meeting."

"Noah, don't torture me like this!" begged David. "Give me the secret now if it's that crucial. Noah . . ."

David heard the familiar click and then hung up the receiver.

Well, I'll lead this project back on the road, he thought. I'll get my team turned around. By the time this project ends, they'll want it to continue on because it ran so well. Even Ted and Sally will thank me.

31

Turn complications into comply-actions

◆

The conference room was full. David entered and sat at the head of the table. All around the table sat his team leads with biting looks on their faces and their arms crossed. Ted sat still, twiddling his thumbs, and looked around the room while whistling to himself. "May I have everybody's attention? That includes yours, too, Ted."

"Yeah, yeah," said Ted.

"Thanks. As you realize, yesterday's meeting was less than successful. Some mistakes were made on my part. I want to ensure that those problems don't resurface. This is a team effort and it cannot succeed without your cooperation. Each one of you were chosen as leads for this project because of your expertise, experience, and knowledge. I would like to tap that background so that we can complete this project successfully.

"Now, I'm passing around today's agenda," continued David. "There's a copy for each of you. You can see that we will discuss problems related to the schedule. Right now, the budget and quality of performance appear good. Also, I'm passing out copies of the reports for your review."

"Are these reports current?" asked Ted.

"Yes," replied David. "They're based on the information received at yesterday's meeting. Starting today, I will collect status inputs prior to Monday's status meeting. Preferably on Friday afternoon at 3 pm. But before I commit to that, let's see if that time poses a problem. Sally?"

"No," said Sally.

"Not at all," chimed Frank.

"Friday? I'd prefer . . ." said Ted.

"I heard he sneaks out early on Fridays," said Sally.

"Mind your own business or I'll . . ." said Ted.

"Let's cut the bickering. Friday, Ted?" asked David.

"Sure, Friday," concurred Ted. "My pleasure."

"Great. I'll generate the new reports and they will be available for our review at Monday's meeting," said David. He made it a point to look at Ted. "That will mean one less meeting so you and the others can concentrate on completing the project. And, I'll get each of you copies of Monday's agenda by Friday so that we all know what's on the table."

"Now you're speaking my language," said Ted.

"He doesn't sound like he's speaking on a fourth grade level," sneered Sally. "Are you going to night school, Ted, and not telling us?"

"Sally, please keep your comments relevant to the project," said David.

"You tell her," said Ted.

"That goes for you, too, Ted," ordered David. "Now, let's address problems with the schedule. Like I said, I need your help in determining what is the best approach to the delivery date slide in the schedule. We can stick to the *status quo* or do something different."

Sally raised her arm and spoke, "Well, I suggest that we reschedule. It seems so much easier than . . ."

"Reschedule?" asked Ted. "You've got to be kidding. That involves more time than we can spare. Besides, my input was accurate."

"So was mine," said Sally.

"Mine, too," agreed Frank. "I don't think we need to reschedule. It's just too early in the project. But working to the *status quo* won't help us either."

"I concur. Rescheduling the project this early on is just too soon. Any ideas as to what can we do to turn things around?" asked David.

"I think that we should concentrate only on the important tasks first and not try to complete everything that's supposed to be done up to this point in time," suggested Ted.

"You mean concentrate on the critical path items only?" asked David.

"Yeah, that's it," said Ted.

"Makes sense," said Sally, nodding her head. "That should bring the project back on schedule. But what about the activities not on the critical path?"

Frank joined the conversation. "Those will slide but they have enough float. As long as the slide is not greater than the float, we don't have to worry about those activities. We'll just do them as we go along."

"What are our other options? Let's brainstorm," said David.

"We could work people overtime," suggested Sally. "Or add more full-time people to our staff. Or hire experienced people part-time. Consultants, I mean. Or we could outsource."

"What's outsourcing?" asked Frank.

"Outsourcing," Sally explained, "is the current buzzword for hiring someone else to do the job because you don't have the requisite skills. But, I'm not so sure . . ."

"Good ideas, but I don't want to put the budget out of whack, too," cautioned David as he interrupted Sally. "It's just not practical. Overtime means higher labour rates and hiring more people, or bringing in consultants will increase overall labour costs."

"We can lower our quality of workmanship. Seems to be the common mode of operation around here, anyway. The activities in the schedule will move along faster," said Ted.

"Can the quality of work by your people get any lower, Ted?" asked Sally.

Ted turned red and picked up a pencil resting on the table. "See this pencil, Sally? You know where you . . ."

David grew tired of the tiffs. "Cut it out. Both of you. You call yourselves professionals, now act professional." He took a deep breath to regain his composure. "Lowering quality will only result in doing a lot of rework and could get us into legal problems. Could you imagine not cleaning the cages completely? The diseases that would spread? The medical bills that would be incurred?"

"It looks like concentrating on the critical path items is the best move we can make. But I can think of only one other thing that could improve schedule performance," said Frank.

"That is?" asked David.

"Better communications," advised Frank. "My people need to know when Ted's people finish their tasks. Likewise for Sally. Sometimes we don't hear when something is done until a day or two later. Terrible communications. How about a call to me, you guys? When you complete an activity that enables my people to begin theirs, could you give me a call? That will help us perform our assigned activities faster. And we're negligent, too. We'll start calling you."

"Sure," said Sally.

"You bet. Just didn't realize that was happening. I guess we were too busy getting our own work in order," said Ted.

"Great. We're making good headway." David then asked, "Is there anything else that we need to address?"

Everyone shook their head.

"Then I'll see everyone next Monday. But remember, my office is always open. I'll be around to pick up status on Friday at 3pm and drop off a copy of Monday's agenda. Take care," said David as he darted from the conference room. I did it, he thought. I had an honest, productive meeting. Noah, you're the greatest.

32

Schedule, budget, and quality can be the cornerstones of the Golden Triangle – or the Bermuda Triangle

◆

David sat behind his desk and reached for the phone. He couldn't resist the urge to tell Noah about how well he did and get the fourth secret. "Noah. It's me."

"Hi me. What's the matter this time?" asked Noah.

"Nothing's the matter."

"Oh, then is this a social call?"

"Noah, I just called to tell you that everything went fine at my meeting. We discussed ways to get back on track. It proved very productive."

"Good for you, David. That's the kind of news I like to hear. How is the Duelling Duo?"

"You mean Ted and Sally?" asked David but expecting no reply. "Well, you can be sure I handled Ted. And Sally, too. I think I communicated to them that I don't like their attitude. After I cleared the stage of their nonsense they both provided constructive ways to improve the performance of the schedule."

"And Frank?"

"Frank had some good suggestions. He mentioned the need to improve communications. The team developed a way to overcome that stumbling block, too."

"Good, good. How's the contingency plan coming along?"

David chuckled. "Yes, Noah, I'm currently updating our contingency plans for handling schedule problems. That way, we will know how to handle related future problems with relative ease."

"Let's get back to the bucks. And I do mean dough."

"No problems with the budget," said David.

"Really?"

The question made David think twice abut the budget. "Right. At least not right now."

"So quality's OK?"

"Nothing with quality." Again, David had to qualify himself. "At least not right now," said David.

"Seems to me you got panicky, thinking that the schedule, budget, and quality were out of whack. Sounds now like you're on your toes. Good going!"

"Noah. I want to know the fourth secret," pleaded David. "You've got to tell me. I'm planning, organizing, and controlling the project. What else is there? Please, I want to know. I've got Craig Yuggenheim visiting soon. Maybe the fourth secret will help me to deal with him. And I'll be better able to lead the project."

Noah released a loud sigh. "You used the secret at this status meeting you're all aglow about. I told you that you would. And you succeeded. So what do you want from me?"

"Come on, Noah. I know you told me that you already revealed the secret to me. But I can't tell hide nor hair what it is."

"It'll come to you. Just did. Smack against your head."

"So I already used it? And successfully, too, at the status meeting? Huh? I still can't figure it out."

"You're leading up to it," said Noah, chuckling.

"What do you mean, I'm leading up to it?" asked David. "You told me that I already know it. And I told you I don't."

"You do."

"I don't."

David heard the click that he had come to know so well.

I don't know about that guy, he thought. Sometimes I think he thinks I'm going to lead this project on my own. He gives me information and then leaves me hanging in mid-air. Crazy guy. He makes absolutely no sense and yet sometimes he makes great sense when he makes no sense!

33

Sometimes you can't with Gantt*

◆

C raig Yuggenheim followed David into the conference room to see the visibility wall. Harrison stood beside them.

"Sir, over here is the project's schedule," said David, pointing to the wall. "I have a copy of the high level bar chart on the wall. If you wish, you can get more detail by looking at the network diagram just below it on the wall here."

"The bar chart doesn't seem to tell me anything," observed Yuggenheim. "Only when the activities are supposed to start and finish. I notice some of the bars in the chart are coloured in, though. What does that mean?"

"That's right, they are," agreed David. "The coloured area indicates that the activity has started and its per cent complete."

"And the completely coloured bars indicate what?" asked Yuggenheim.

David smiled and said, "That they are 100 per cent complete."

"So as you can see, the project is progressing nicely," interjected Harrison.

"I have a slight qualification to that remark, sir," said David.

"Oh?" asked Yuggenheim.

"Some of the activities on the critical path, reflected in the network diagram, have slid," said David.

"Meaning?" asked Yuggenheim. He removed a yellow silk handkerchief and wiped the perspiration from his forehead.

"Meaning that we are behind schedule," explained David. "That is, if we continue at the current pace we will not make the project completion date that you requested." His finger then pointed to the last activity in the network.

"But you've managed to take care of that, haven't you?" asked Yuggenheim.

David noticed Harrison's head nodding to tell the young executive how to respond.

* Another word for bar chart is Gantt chart, named after the originator Henry Gantt back in the early 1890s.

"Yes, indeed. In our last status meeting we developed ways to get back on schedule. I'm confident, and so are the others, that we'll be back on schedule by the next status meeting, which is in a week," said David.

"Tell Mr. Yuggenheim about the budget," ordered Harrison.

"Yes, the budget. That's my next question," said Yuggenheim.

"Glad you brought that up. Let's walk over here to where you can see the budget report posted on the wall," said David. He led both men to it. "We are right on target in terms of what was supposed to be spent and what was actually spent up to the last status review meeting."

"I keep a close watch on the monies spent, right David?" asked Harrison.

"Yes, you do, sir," said David.

"Very good. Now explain to me what else you have on this wall," said Yuggenheim, sweeping his arm in front of him and putting his handkerchief away.

"Well, over here we have an organization chart. It shows me as the project manager, my leads, and the people reporting to them," explained David.

"I don't see me listed here. Where am I shown?" asked Harrison.

David visually inspected the chart. "Sorry sir. Must be a slight oversight. I'll revise the chart to show that I'm reporting to you."

Harrison responded with a chilly "Thank you."

"And what is this?" asked Yuggenheim.

"That's the printout of the work breakdown structure. It shows all the tasks and subtasks required to complete the project," said David.

"And this?" asked Yuggenheim.

"It's a copy of the statement of understanding. That's posted for anyone to review in order to keep refreshed about what the project wants to achieve and under what parameters," said David.

"I see," said Yuggenheim. "And this map?"

"It's a map of the zoo," blurted Harrison. "That was my idea."

"Oh really?" asked Yuggenheim.

"Yes," said David. He tried to avoid a potential rift between himself and his boss. "It helps us to resolve any communication problems about what's where."

"And this?" asked Yuggenheim, pointing to the lower right portion of the wall.

"That's a catch-all or miscellaneous section of reports and other documents that people may want to look at from time to time," said David.

Yuggenheim took a panoramic view of the wall by stepping back. "This wall is quite interesting. You call it a visibility wall? Well, now I see why. No pun intended."

David knew he had made points with Yuggenheim. "When holding status meetings and other sessions here, we can conveniently refer to it to resolve any difficulties."

"You're doing quite a fine job, gentlemen. I'm impressed. I'll call my family and tell them that you people have everything under control," said Yuggenheim.

"Thank you, sir," said David.

Harrison nodded his head. "Great. I'll keep a watchful eye on everything for you."

"You do that," said Yuggenheim. "Got to go." He walked out of the conference room.

Harrison turned to David and said "Mr. Yuggenheim, I mean Craig, means it when he says we're doing a fine job. I think we can be proud of how we're doing."

"I don't know what I'd do without your guidance and leadership," answered David, following Yuggenheim's footsteps. Closing the door behind him, he smiled as he stepped away from the conference room leaving Harrison alone.

34

Accentuate the positive but don't ignore the negative

◆

The team leads sat around the conference table. David started the meeting. "I've received everyone's status and the latest set of schedules I have just distributed reflects it. As you can see, we're back on schedule."

"I know I am," said Ted.

"Are you sure, Teddy?" asked Sally.

Ted pointed a finger at her. "Just remember, I may be your boss someday. So watch it."

"Ted, you must be smoking something," said Sally.

"Look, cut it out. Please," said Frank.

"Thank you, Frank," said David, amazed at Frank's assertiveness. "Let's keep on track, everyone. We can now work on following the schedule without just concentrating on the critical path items. Turn to the budget report."

"Wow!" exclaimed Ted.

"My God!" screamed Sally.

"I don't believe it!" said Frank.

"I do. The cost estimate for completing the project at the current pace is higher than we can allow. Got to do something. Sally, any ideas?" asked David.

"We could cut back staff," suggested Sally.

"That won't work. I'm already resource poor," said Ted.

"Me, too. It's just not practical," added Frank.

"I agree. What about using less expensive contractors to do the manual labour?" asked David. "We might be able to cut the costs there."

"Yeah, I could do that. I heard that another firm is cheaper and its reputation is better," said Frank.

"Then why haven't we used them before?" asked Ted.

"Because we've been using the existing contractor for years. That's all. It's been convenient, but costly," said Frank.

"How about getting on to it right away?" asked David.

"You bet," said Frank.

"Since we're talking about costs, I think we can rent more reasonably priced equipment to tear down cages and buildings and haul away debris. The current rental service is expensive and often untimely. I think I know of a better place," said Ted.

"Please get on to it right away, Ted. What else can we do?" asked David.

"We can reduce overtime. Some of us, including myself, have been working longer than eight hours a day," said Sally.

"Was overtime necessary for what you did?" asked David.

"In order to remove the schedule slide it was," noted Sally. "We also have some additional overtime coming up."

Frank agreed. "We do too."

"Likewise for my group," said Ted.

"I suggest, then, that unless the work pertains to a critical path activity there will be no overtime permitted," said David. "Agreed?"

"Makes sense," said Ted as he shook his head. "Some of my people complete the critical path tasks first during regular hours and work on the noncritical path tasks in the evening. That is, before we had the major schedule slide."

"Same for me," added Frank.

"Then let's cease overtime for all noncritical activities for the remainder of the project," ordered David. "Any other ideas?"

"Yes. I've noticed that we have rental equipment lying around, not being used," said Sally.

Ted slammed his fist on the table. "That's poppycock!"

"No it isn't," snapped Sally. "I've seen trucks and diggers sitting unused. And not just once in a while, either."

"Oh really?" asked David. "Well, that's got to cease, too. If something is not being used, then return it. Those costs add up, especially if they're not being used for days at a time. Good. Some more suggestions."

"Maybe we can spend some money to save money," said Frank.

"Huh?" asked David.

"That's what I've been telling my husband for years," said Sally.

"Poor man," said Ted.

"Please, contain yourselves," said David, looking right at Ted and Sally. "What's your idea, Frank?"

Frank coughed and then spoke. "I suggest that we rent, lease with the option to buy, or outright purchase walkie-talkies, cellular phones, CB-radios, or beepers for some of the staff working out in the zoo grounds.

"A few of my people spend half their time running back to the office building to get tools or answers to questions," continued Frank. "With a portable communication device they can just dial up and get the answers without having to spend travel time back and forth. Also, they can get someone to deliver the needed tools. We could complete most tasks in less time and even reduce labour costs because less people are working on the task. In the end, we're streamlining our operations."

"Great idea, Frank. What do you folks think?" asked David.

"Many of my people have experienced the same problem," said Ted.

"Mine, too," said Sally.

"Let's go for it. Give me your requirements for communication devices by the next status meeting, and I'll put together a cost analysis. We'll have a team review of it and decide what looks best. Then off to purchasing it goes. I'll expedite the order, so we'll have the equipment pretty quick," said David. "Are there any other ideas? Questions? Comments?"

Everyone shook their heads.

"Great. See everyone next time," said David as he packed his material and headed out of the conference room. Even though he considered the meeting successful, he felt troubled by a lingering problem. He knew that he had to take action soon or the project would fail to finish on time or within budget.

35

Avoiding conflict leads to conflict

◆

David reached for the phone on his desk to make a call to someone he had contacted many times before. "Noah, it's me again. I need to talk with you."

An unmistakable voice came on the line. "It's 7pm. It's earlier than the last time you called me, but it's still . . ."

"I know it's seven o'clock at night. But I've got a problem," persisted David.

"Don't we all. OK, we haven't talked in a good while," said Noah.

"Thanks," said David. "This one is turning serious. It's jeopardizing my whole project."

"Let me guess. Your schedule slid . . . into the next decade, and you don't . . ."

"No, it's not another schedule slide. And I think we've got the budget overrun under control," explained David. "It's another problem. One that I wish went away."

"I know what it is."

"You do?"

"Sure, David. It's something that most project managers choose to ignore, but only at their own peril."

"You know what it is? Just out of curiosity share it with me, Noah."

"Morale," snapped Noah. "You've got morale problems. And I suspect the major culprits are Sally and Ted."

"Detective Noah, you're right on! How in the world did you know?"

"I realized it when I eavesdropped on your first status meeting."

David sighed. "I've tried to ignore the problem, but it's getting worse. Intolerable in fact. Their fighting is getting more frequent and vocal at meetings. Downright insulting. I know its impacting the project. But what am I to do?"

"You've taken a good first step. And that's to recognize that a problem exists and not choosing to ignore it."

"OK, so I know that a problem exists. And I choose to fix it," said David. "Now what?"

"Now fix it."

"That's the next step? Fix it?" asked David.

"A lot of project managers pretend that it will go away, David. They respond by doing nothing."

"And then?"

"And then things only get worse. Step back and analyse the situation. That way you can remain objective about what's going on."

"You say step back and analyse the situation?" asked David. A few seconds passed and then he spoke. "Well I know that Ted says something and Sally makes a negative comment. So maybe it's Sally's fault," said David.

"It's nobody's fault," corrected Noah. "Faulting lays blame and causes tensions to increase. Take a more positive approach."

"Then what you are saying is that I should investigate the source of the problem and not look for someone to pinpoint," said David. "Makes sense. I do remember Ted being the wise-cracker in the beginning, not Sally. You're right. It's not something simple like pointing to someone. It's not black and white but shades of grey. Well, what's the next step?"

"I give up. What is the next step?"

"All right, I'll figure it out," retorted David. "I'll meet with Ted and Sally individually and get their sides of the story."

Noah explained. "There are advantages of having private meetings. You meet one-to-one without outside interference. And you get the benefits of sharing insights while gaining a closeness not realized by a group effort."

"Is there anything else I need to do?"

"I'll tell you what to do. Hold the meetings, give me a call, and maybe we'll meet to discuss the results," said Noah. "Besides, we haven't seen each other for a while."

"OK, I'll meet with each one the first thing in the morning. Care to attend?" asked David.

"No. You're on your own. You're a big boy now."

David heard the familiar click on the phone line.

I just wanted to ask him one more question, thought David. What that fourth secret is. All I'm asking is for a little understanding and some leadership. Maybe next time.

36

Have you talked with, not to, a team member today?

◆

Sally walked into the conference room ahead of David. They sat next to each other. David had deliberately sat next to her, rather than across from her, to avoid an adversarial atmosphere. "Sally, I'm glad we have the opportunity to talk with each other."

"Must be something important," she said. "This is the first time this has ever happened."

"Yeah, it's been a madhouse since we've started on this project."

"You can say that again, David. Seems like everything has been turned topsy-turvy."

David shrugged. "I just want to say that I appreciate the fine job you and your people have been doing. I think that, since the first week of this project, not one scheduled activity that your people were responsible for has slid. And you've operated well within the budget. Great work."

"Thank you. So why this meeting?"

David had a slight cough and then spoke. "Well, there's a conflict between you and another team member that has impeded the overall performance of the project."

"Oh?"

"Come on, Sally, you know who I'm talking about."

"Ted?"

He nodded his head. "That's right, Ted. It seems that at every meeting we have you two start arguing and going at each other like pit-bull terriers. The meetings turn into a mental battle of wits rather than a meaningful session. The conflict raises the tension level to such a point that sometimes any chance of meaningful discussions is impossible. I'd like it to cease."

"Well, if you think it's me who's starting it, you better think twice," she said, with her voice rising in anger.

"Sally, I'm not blaming anyone," he assured. "I just want to find out the cause of the problem before it really impacts the project. Please. I need your cooperation."

"You are receiving it. You've just said that our group's performance is great. As long as we deliver, what do you care about my relationship with Ted?"

"Because it affects the performance of the rest of the team, that's why. We're all part of the same team. We need to work together if we expect to finish the project on time and at a satisfactory level of quality. You do want to achieve those results, don't you?" asked David.

"Sure. You bet I do."

"OK, then tell me why you and Ted tangle so much. I'll keep everything in this conversation in the strictest confidence," he said.

Sally adjusted her position in the chair and took a deep breath. "Well, for openers, Ted makes sexist remarks and I don't like it. I know from colleagues that he feels that I am where I'm at because I'm a woman. It burns him even more that I'm 11 years younger than he is."

"Any other reasons?" asked David.

"Yes," continued Sally. "He thinks that my group has all the best equipment and the best assignments on this project. True, we have the same number of people with about the same skill levels, but he agreed to the responsibility matrix. He could have said something then. There's one last thing."

"What's that?"

"He thinks you and I are ganging up on him. He told a friend of mine that the other day."

"Ganging up on him?" he asked. That was the first time he ever heard that. "I don't understand."

She explained. "Well, he felt that he should have been selected as the project manager. And he also thinks that I still have an interest in the position, which I don't. I heard that he believes that you will leave before the project is over and that it will be either him or myself who will occupy the position."

David fell back in his chair. "I'm not leaving, unless I'm asked to. And it doesn't look like that's going to happen. As for my replacement, if something like that is necessary there's no guarantee who will take over the position. None. That's completely up to my boss. So let's close the book on that one. Look, I want to thank you for your candid revelations about these differences between you and Ted. I promise you everything said here will remain confidential. I hope you can put aside these differences." He looked right into her eyes. "Can you?"

"Well, he has to be just as willing." David rose from the table with Sally following. They headed towards the exit.

"Thanks again for your candour," he said. "I know I can count on your support during the next status meeting."

After Sally had left the area, David headed towards Ted's office.

37

Encourage people to shine, not whine

◆

David knocked on the glass office door. "Ted? Got a minute?"

"Yeah, sure," said Ted. He had his face buried in a pile of papers.

"I'd like to talk with you about something that I think is a very serious problem," said David. He noticed that Ted continued working without looking up.

"Oh? Have a seat." Ted kept working on a document.

David spoke. "I want to mention first of all that you and your people have been doing a fine job."

Ted stopped his work and looked at David. "They always do. So?"

"I mean it sincerely."

"Yeah, so do I. Now tell me the bad news so I can get back to work on the project."

"All right, Ted," said David. He shifted himself in the chair so as to look straight at Ted. "I'll be direct with you. Do you hold a grudge against me? Let's put it out on the table right now."

Ted leaned back in his chair and shook his head. "No, no, no. I've got nothing against you."

"Then why the negative attitude?"

Ted shrugged his shoulders. "Negative attitude? Where? When?"

"Like now. And at the staff meetings. Quite frankly Ted, I'm tired of it. So are some of the others."

"All right, all right," said Ted, nodding his head. "Look, I'll admit that I've not been too pleasant."

"Why?"

"Why? Well, for one I wanted the job that you've got."

You can't get more direct than that, thought David. "Ted, I know you've been a project manager in the past."

"Yeah."

"And that has given you a great amount of knowledge and experience that proves useful to the success of this project, right?" asked David.

"Yeah."

"It's imperative, then, that we receive your support and cooperation."

"But my people have performed well. We meet most of our scheduled milestones."

"No quarrel with that," assured David. "But it's the spirit in the way it's being done. A rift has developed between you and Sally and between your people and hers."

"Really?"

"Come on, Ted. You know well enough that there is a rift," said David with a mild chuckle. "And it's got to close. Now. Eighty per cent of the tasks on the critical path are your people's tasks and half of those require the joint participation of Sally's people."

Ted nodded his head. "You're right. It's got to close. But the other side has to make an effort, too. And you know women. You can't live with them and you can't shoot them."

"Now wait a minute, Ted. It's comments like that that make the rift even wider. You make that sort of comment at meetings. And it gets Sally angry."

"Brings out the real woman in her."

"Her wrath, to be specific. It must stop. Now. Will you give me your word that you will stop?" asked David. He looked directly into Ted's eyes.

Ted sighed deeply. "All right, I'll admit I've dug at her a little. I'll stop it."

"Good," said David, smiling.

Ted raised his finger in the air. "But if she wants to be treated as an equal, she'd better work under the same conditions as my people."

"What do you mean?"

Ted explained. "I mean that my people get a chance to use the quality of equipment Sally and her people use. Our equipment is technologically out-of-date and less often than not in good working order. Gets my people angry every time, and I can't say I blame them."

"I see, I was unaware of that but I'll look into it. Any other concerns?" asked David.

"None worth mentioning. Look, I don't mean to be unreasonable, but you can see I've got a right to share in the wealth here too."

David made a point of telling rather than asking Ted: "I'd like for you and Sally to resolve your differences. Not for my sake, but for the sake of the project. And our conversation is strictly confidential. I am not interested in others knowing that we've talked. And I feel that now that you've expressed your feelings I can better lead our team to success."

"I see."

"So, in light of our remarks, I'd like to see a change in your attitude towards the project and Sally at the next status meeting. Agreed?" asked David.

"Sure."

"Great. Thanks for your time," said David. He proffered his hand. He felt Ted's tight grip for the first time. "Keep up the good work and see you at the next status meeting." Then David left Ted's office.

38

You need problem-identifiers as well as problem-solvers

◆

Ted, Sally, Frank, and David sat around the conference table. David put a copy of the agenda on the overhead projector screen and flipped the on switch. Each of the attendees had already received a copy before the meeting so as to be prepared.

"The first order of business is the schedule. As you can see, based upon everyone's input, we've slid on the critical path. That means we've slid our completion date with only two months to go," observed David. "Ted, any comments regarding your items in the schedule?"

Ted spoke, but softly. "Two of my activities on the critical path have slid. I . . ."

"I must interject something," said Sally.

Oh boy, here come the fireworks, thought David. "Go ahead."

"The slide is not attributed to anything that Ted's group has done," said Sally. "My people failed to deliver the equipment when Ted's people needed it."

Ted smiled and said, "Well, I'll be . . ."

"Why? Why did they fail to deliver the equipment on time?" asked David, somewhat amazed.

Sally explained. "Well, the two men using it thought they had to return it to the rental agency. Not until after they returned it did they review the work order and realize that it was to be delivered to Ted's people. Sorry, Ted. My *faux pas*."

"You . . . There's nothing to apologize for, Sally. I wish someone would have notified me or my people, though," said Ted.

"My people were afraid you'd get mad. So I guess they just sort of forgot about it. I only discovered the real reason this morning. And I chewed them out for it. I assure you, it won't happen again," said Sally, smiling.

Ted beamed a smile back. "Sounds to me you've got the problem under control. I know I can count on your cooperation," said Ted.

David did not want to lose this moment so he smiled, too, and looked at

Frank. "Frank, any comments about your status? Looks like you've slid a few activities, two of which happen to be on the critical path."

Frank looked sullen as he spoke. "We've had some staff turnover. Three people handed in their two-week notice after getting jobs elsewhere. People are getting nervous, you know, as we come closer to the project completion date. Most of them fear they'll be out of a job. They doubt the Yuggenheims' offer of employment with one of their other firms is for real."

"I was afraid of that," remarked David. "And Sally, care to comment on the status of your activities?"

"I'm having the same problem as Frank. People are getting nervous. Although no one in my group has jumped ship, one person I know of is looking for another job," explained Sally. "You know half of my people are working on critical path activities. I think I'll need to hire temporary help to complete my remaining piece of the project."

"I can help alleviate this problem," said Ted.

David turned to face Ted. "How's that, Ted?"

"I can loan some of my people to Frank and Sally. Many of my tasks are within a few days of completion. I don't want to have some people sitting around idle and spreading rumours, like the Yuggenheims' are backing out on their promise of employment with one of their firms. These people are active and want to be productive. You remember Sattingler's Law: It works better if you plug it in. And by not plugging them in you can bring the morale down quite low and productivity with it," said Ted.

"Great," said Frank with a grin. "I'll need six people for five days within the next three days."

"I can spare two," said Ted.

"I can spare one," added Sally.

"But that adds up to only three. I need three more. I'll have to hire some temporary workers but they'll cost more, especially now that I'll need them on such short notice," noted Frank.

"Wait a minute," said David as he held his right hand up. "Ordinarily that sounds like a logical solution. But there's one other problem for which we haven't accounted."

"Oh?" asked Sally.

"Really?" inquired Ted.

"What is it?" joined Frank.

David released a light cough. "We've got a budget slide with our schedule slide. As you can see in the budget report, we're projected to finish 27 per cent above the original estimate to complete the project. Any additional costs could prove disastrous. We'll finish but we'll miss our target."

"Sounds like a state-of-the-nation with a combination of inflation and recession," said Frank.

"It's more like choosing between guns and butter. I'm at a loss," stated David, placing his face in his hands. He then looked up at everyone. "I have no idea how to turn this situation around. I checked the contingency plans we've put together but we never accounted for this circumstance. Let's break for five minutes and sort of mull it over. And when we come back, we'll finish up this meeting."

David left the conference room and entered his office. He reached for the phone on his desk. "Hello, Noah. I need to see you right away. Got another mess."

"No, I don't have another mess. I try to keep a clean place," said Noah with a chuckle.

"Seriously, I have another mess. Quit teasing," said David.

"You mean another fine mess you've got me into?"

"Yes, another one," admitted David. "Can I see you at our usual meeting place in 15 minutes? Please?" asked David.

"Let me check my schedule." Several seconds of silence passed. "OK. Fifteen minutes."

"Great. I'll see you then," said David. David hung up the phone and raced back to the conference room.

"Something's come up. I have to go. We'll reconvene this meeting tomorrow morning at 8am. Anybody have a problem with this time?"

Everyone shook their head.

"What do we do in the meantime? Business as usual?" asked Ted.

"Yeah?" asked Sally.

"Just let the schedule slide and burn money?" asked Frank.

"No. Of course not, said David, letting out a sigh. "The sharing of those three people will suffice for now. Also consider hiring temporary employees but only as a last resort. But we still have eight weeks to finish this project and I feel we can do it within budget and on schedule. Think of other ideas. Until tomorrow let's just keep cool. See you all then."

David then rushed from the conference room.

39

Everything on a project incurs a cost, monetary or otherwise

◆

Noah was sitting on a bench. David sat next to him, noticing that the old man seemed more preoccupied with feeding the pigeons and smoking his pipe than this meeting. "Noah, I'm sure glad you could make it."

Noah broke out of his trance. "Oh, it's you. So you have an emergency?"

David released a nervous laugh. "You bet it's an emergency. A heck of a one, too. I've got a real problem."

"Don't we all. So how can I help you?"

"I need some ideas," said David. "All your ideas have been great. And now I need another really great one."

"You came up with a lot of the ideas, they weren't all mine."

"All right, I won't argue that I thought up most of them on my own. But you helped me derive them. That's what I meant," said David.

"What's your problem?" Noah stopped feeding the pigeons and puffed on his pipe.

"Well, the problem is that I'm facing a double-edged sword," said David.

"I always knew that you were a sharp guy."

"But it's sharp at both ends! I have a schedule slide and a budget overrun," added David. "What do I do?"

"You also had a communication problem. What's its status?"

"I think I've effectively solved the problem between Ted and Sally. They seem to be making an effort to resolve their differences. That will help in the future. Unfortunately their tiff probably contributed to this predicament," said David.

Noah started stroking his long grey beard as he smoked his pipe. "Did you meet with them to discuss the problem?"

"That's right," replied David. "I met with them both individually. Seems there were some misunderstandings on everyone's part. In fact, the status review meeting we held today was the smoothest we've ever had."

"Good. Did you brainstorm any alternative solutions to this new problem?"

"Yes, we did generate some ideas for overcoming this problem. We have a partial solution."

"Not a complete solution?"

"That's right," answered David with a red face. "It's incomplete. We can share labour resources. I guess you can call it an attempt at resource levelling."

"That's nice. But it sounds to me like it's a short-term solution."

"I know it's a short-term solution. But you have to give me credit – in the past I dealt with some difficult issues and handled them well," said David.

"Here here," said Noah. "There's no need to get defensive."

"But we're all at a loss for what we can do next. It seems that if we implement any solution a trade-off occurs," explained David as he threw his arms up into the air.

Noah adjusted his cap and took a deep drag from his pipe. "Are you familiar with the term TANSTAAFL?"

"TANSTAAFL? What in the world is that?" asked David.

"It's an acronym and stands for There Ain't No Such Thing As A Free Lunch. Get the picture?"

David took a deep breath. "I'm beginning to see your point. Nothing ever comes free. That means that we are going to have to sacrifice something in the short run in order to gain in the long run."

"This world is one of trade-offs. Mao Tse-tung summed it up pretty well."

"What did Chairman Mao say?" asked David.

"Mao said that sometimes you have to take two steps backwards in order to move three steps forwards."

"OK, then that means I'll have to make some type of trade-off decision. Well, my leads and I will figure something out," said David. "Unless, of course, you want to give us an answer now?"

"You and your leads push forward. You'll get to where you want to go."

"I already get your gist. You want me to figure it out for myself. OK, I'll accept that. You've already given me a clue."

"Then play Sherlock Holmes," snapped Noah.

"Well . . ." said David, combing his hair with his fingers. "I can eliminate the use of any unnecessary resources, especially on noncritical tasks. That's one way to reduce costs."

"And?"

"I can reassign more reasonably priced resources from noncritical activities to more critical ones. Then I can let the more expensive ones go."

"Remember TANSTAAFL," warned Noah.

"Yeah, I'll just have to make sure that those noncritical resources can complete the critical tasks. What else?"

"I'll ask the questions," said Noah, chuckling.

"I'll look at the schedule and readjust it, if possible. I suspect that switching the logic a little will reduce flow time and may even lead to using fewer resources. That would help bring the schedule and budget into sync with each other."

"And?"

"I've got it!" barked David. "I'll analyse our work processes and determine faster, more effective ways to run the project. We may have some redundant activities in a few areas that can be eliminated. And, we'll redeploy those people currently working on noncritical tasks. Noah, I could kiss you."

"Keep your distance, sonny," warned Noah, pushing his arms out and backing off.

"Just teasing. But I want to know something. You owe it to me," said David.

"Just as you don't owe me anything, I don't owe you anything," said Noah. He put his right hand into the watch pocket of his jeans, pulled out an old pocket watch with foreign writing on it, looked at it, and then put it away. "That way, you don't feel obligated. You do something for someone because you want to."

"OK. So do you want to tell me the fourth secret?" asked David.

"How can I tell you something you already know?"

"What do you mean I already know it? Noah, I wouldn't be asking you if I did. What is it?"

"Hindsight always provides 20–20 vision."

David grew impatient. He felt a strange urge to place his hands around Noah's neck and squeeze the answer out. "I can't wait until the project is over. I have to take action now. I've got to proact rather than react to the situation. I need to keep my people motivated, to give them direction. They need my support, damn it, not me getting in the way of doing their jobs."

"I'm very pleased and proud of you. Even though you probably want to strangle me."

David turned red from having such guilty thoughts. "Proud of me? For what? I've had nothing but problems."

"But we all have problems. It's how we cope with them that distinguishes the men from the boys." Noah blew rings of smoke.

"All right, I'll admit every project has its problems," said David nodding his head. "And this one seems to have its share. Up to this point in time, we've managed to solve all of them."

"We?" asked Noah. He stopped blowing circles. "We?"

"I meant 'we,' meaning myself and my team."

"I'm very proud of you."

"Well, I can see I'm not getting anywhere. My project is falling apart and you're telling me you're proud of me," said David as he rose from the bench.

"Perspective. You've got to maintain perspective. And remain detached. Stay objective, not emotional. It helps to get a grasp on the big picture," said Noah. He started feeding the pigeons.

"You bet I'll concentrate on the total picture. Good day!" said David, walking away.

40

The solutions lie within ourselves, not in the stars

◆

"I think we have some solutions to our problem of a schedule slide and budget overrun," said David as he fell back into his chair. He felt the stare of perplexed faces from Ted, Sally, and Frank, who were sitting around the conference table.

"Oh?" asked Ted.

"Well, what is it?" asked Sally.

"Yeah, what?" asked Frank.

"The way I see it we have several options and there may be others, so please speak up if you think of them."

"Go on," said Ted.

"We can eliminate any unnecessary resources," said David.

"Like what?" asked Frank.

"Ted, do you have any forklifts that you're contracting but not using?" asked David.

"Yeah, there are some forklifts we're paying for but not using. Hmmm," said Ted, rubbing his chin. "I'll check our contracts with the rental agency. I'm pretty sure that we can cancel those without a penalty. We've been renting the vehicles on a daily basis."

"Good." David turned to Sally. "What about in your department?"

"We have some contract people but . . ."

"But what, Sally?" pressured David.

"Well . . . we may need them some time in the future."

"Is that what the schedule indicates?" asked David as he looked up at the network diagram pinned across the wall.

"Not exactly. I guess I can let them go. It's just that it's hard to get good, reliable contract people and to have them available when you need them."

"TANSTAAFL," blurted David.

"What?" the others all said at the same time.

"TANSTAAFL," repeated David. "It's an acronym, and it means There Ain't No Such Thing As A Free Lunch. I said it because we're going to have to lose them to cut costs. Now, we have some other options."

"What are they?" asked Ted.

"We can readjust the schedule," said Ted. "Any ideas?"

A short silence ensued followed by a burst of energy.

"You know," said Ted, snapping his fingers, "why couldn't we handle the dismantling of the concession stands during the same time as tearing apart the monkey cages? That would reduce the flowtime considerably for the overall project."

David viewed the histograms on the wall. "That wouldn't make these people work that much more than they currently are." He looked at Frank and Sally.

"Not a bad idea," observed Sally. "The time required of my people handling those tasks concurrently would increase slightly from four hours a day to five."

"I agree," said Frank. "That would also allow my people to concentrate on other critical tasks."

"Great," said David. "Now we have one other way to reduce costs and get back on schedule. I just can't remember what it is."

"Did it have to do with automation?" asked Ted.

"No," replied David.

"Reducing our workload?" asked Frank.

Ted shook his head.

"Working differently?" asked Sally.

"That's it," said David, hitting his fist upon the table. "We need to look at the way we're doing business."

"You mean work smarter, not harder," blurted Frank.

"Exactly," said David. "Any ideas?"

The long silence returned.

"We handle too much paperwork," snapped Ted.

"What do you mean?" asked David.

"Well, we have Sally filling out project completion sheets. I complete a set, and so does Frank. Then, you compile them. Maybe we can minimize the effort. It takes me a half a day to fill out those damn forms."

"A full day for me," said Sally. "And I use two people to help me."

"Likewise for me," joined Frank.

"OK. Any suggestions?" asked David.

"Let's take someone from a noncritical activity to do the work. That way we can concentrate on doing the work and not tie up any more people than we have to," suggested Ted."

"Right on," said Sally.

"I agree," said Frank.

"Sounds good to me. I'll work out the details with you guys later. Any other ideas?"

"Not from me," said Sally.

"Or me," said Frank.

"Ditto for me," added Ted.

"Then we're down to the wire, folks," said David, rising from his chair. "Let's make it happen."

41

Whisper a loud secret and everyone will hear it

◆

"Noah, you've got to see what's happening!" said David over the phone.

"See what?"

"The miracle that's occurring. I can't believe it myself. It's all working. Everything you told me."

"Then you've mastered all four of the secrets of practical project management."

"But I know only three of them. Tell me the fourth one. This project's on a roll."

"You know it already. You just don't realize it."

"Damn it, Noah. Stop pulling my leg. How do I know that I haven't missed it completely?" asked David, as he felt the anxiety move up his spine. "It could make the difference between success and failure."

Noah coughed lightly and the level of his voice dropped. "You're right. Without the fourth secret, all else will fail and mean nothing."

"Then tell me."

"Tell you what, I'll meet you at your office in 30 minutes and we'll see if you know the fourth secret."

"A deal. Then, you'll tell me?" asked David.

The only reply was the familiar click on the other end of the telephone line.

A shadow appeared in the corridor, and with it the sweet-smelling aroma of pipe smoke.

"Noah, it's good . . . no great . . . to see you. Tell me the fourth secret," said David rushing toward the open door.

"Patience, boy. You're dealing with an elder."

"Sorry."

"Not as much as I am. Give me the tour. I don't have all day," said Noah.

"Right this way to the conference room," said David, leading the way.

They entered the conference room. Noah took a seat while David stood, directing the conversation.

"As you know, we hold all our meetings here in the conference room. We review the schedule and budget to ensure compliance and so everyone knows what they're supposed to do, when and where. We focus on the critical path, and everyone makes suggestions for improving the performance if anything on the critical path slides."

"How are Sally and Ted getting along?" asked Noah.

"Great. They seem to have placed their differences aside and have concentrated on the vision of what we hope to achieve."

A smile came to Noah's face, the kind that a proud father has after his child does something successfully for the first time.

"Are you listening, Noah?" asked David.

"Yes, and so have you been, sonny."

"Huh? Anyway, we're now down to the wire. I've been walking around the zoo to verify the feedback that I receive from the team members. I want to ensure that everyone moves in the right direction according to our plans."

"You keep this up and I just might adopt you as my son."

"You approve so far?"

Noah rose from his seat. "I couldn't ask for more, sonny."

"There's more," added David. "I make sure that communication moves up and down the chain of command. That's so the right hand, so to speak, knows what the left hand is doing. Everyone must be appraised of the situation."

"Talk is cheap. Show me."

"OK, follow me," said David.

Noah did just that with an even wider grin.

Outside the young executive and Noah stood watching as the hippotami were herded from the artificial lake and into the caged wagon.

David looked at his watch. "Right on schedule."

"Brings back memories," said Noah. "Is that all?"

"Are you kidding, Noah? This activity is occurring simultaneously throughout the zoo. Look, over there."

Noah turned.

"It's Ted and Sally. Remember them?"

Noah nodded his head.

Both Ted and Sally approached them.

"Who let this crazy-looking old guy in?" asked Ted.

"This is a friend of mine," said David. "His name is . . ."

"Why you little whipper snapper," replied Noah. "If I was in charge I'd . . ."

"Let's just drop it, you guys," said David. "What's the issue?"

Noah stood with his arms crossed, listening but giving Ted the evil eye.

"We need to resolve a problem," said Sally. "We need to herd the elephants, but we just don't have enough wagons to carry them off. We could delay the herding of the giraffes and use their wagon but that would cause a slide on the schedule."

"I see," said David, stroking his chin with his right hand. "Do you two have any ideas?"

"Ah, yeah . . ." said Ted.

"We discussed them but we didn't decide which one because you're the leader of this project," snapped Sally.

"And if I wasn't around to make the decision what would you do?" asked David, glancing at Noah.

Noah dropped his arms and his scowl turned into a grin.

"We'd have to resolve it ourselves," said Ted.

"Then do just that," commanded David. "And let me know what you decide. I'll help you in any way I can."

Ted and Sally marched off, discussing between themselves the best solution to resolve the problem.

"I don't like him," snapped Noah.

"Nobody does, but I can't let that interfere with getting the project done," said David. "Teamwork is absolutely essential and I have to make sure that it happens."

"Well, you certainly did that," observed Noah. "I am especially pleased how you encourage initiative and collaboration between those two. I couldn't have done a better job myself, encouraging teamwork between such difficult personalities."

"OK, Noah," said David, looking his mentor straight in the eyes. "Tell me the fourth secret. I need to know."

"I don't have to," said Noah. He turned and walked away.

"Noah, don't play games. You promised."

"I already did and you showed it to me," said Noah.

"You did? I did?" asked David as he stretched out his arms.

"It came to you like a whisper in the night and it's being shouted everywhere around here. Got to go, sonny."

He heard Ted and Sally's voices yelling something about making their decision and for him not to go away. David turned briefly around to see from what direction they were coming. He then turned towards Noah.

But Noah was gone.

42

Building a team is more than assembling a group of people

◆

Aband played jazz music in the background. Several rows of round tables were adorned with decorative dinnerware and ice buckets crammed with champagne bottles. Employees of the zoo sat at each table. One long table, divided in half by a podium, faced these tables. David sat on one side along with Harrison, Ted, Sally, and Frank. The Yuggenheim family sat at the other end.

Craig Yuggenheim was giving his congratulatory speech ". . . and furthermore, ladies and gentlemen, I think that the zoo dismantling project would never have come under budget and on time and with so little trouble if it hadn't been for the leadership of one individual, David Michaels. Let's give him some applause."

David rose from his seat and came to the podium. "Thank you, thank you all. You know, it's nice to complete a project on such pleasant results. The animals have been sent to other good zoos. Not one animal has died or become ill from the trauma of the move. The Habeas Corporation has moved ahead and begun building on the zoo premises. Each and every one of us has a new and higher-paying position with one of the many successful Yuggenheim firms . . ."

"Don't forget it wouldn't have happened without my cooperation," blurted Ted.

"Shut up, Ted, and let him finish his speech," said Sally.

"Yeah, I agree with Sally," joined Frank.

Ted took the bait, "Listen, babe . . ."

David continued, "As I was saying, we all gained from the project. I know that Ted's cooperation was critical . . ."

"Oh really?" glared Sally.

". . . but so was everyone else's. And that cooperation proved essential toward the end of the project when we faced a double-edged sword. Translated that means we were behind schedule and we exceeded our budget. But, we managed to pull through . . ." David coughed several times in an attempt to clear his throat. ". . . due to the leadership of Harrison Farnsworth." Some weak applause came from the audience. Harrison rose from his chair, took a bow and then sat down.

"Ladies and gentlemen, if we hadn't concentrated on meeting the schedule first and then the budget, we'd still be working on the project today. But through your cooperation . . ." As David spoke, he noticed that Noah stood far across the ballroom at its entrance. David cracked a smile. ". . . and the knowledge and willingness to share that with others, this project would never have ended on time and within budget and at a level of quality that we all can be proud of." Loud applause filled the ballroom.

"In closing, I'd like to share three . . . no four . . . secrets with you. These four secrets are so fundamental that we sometimes take them for granted and never implement them.

"The first secret is planning. Every project needs a gameplan on how it is going to proceed. We need to know our goal, the steps to achieve it, the order those steps take, and when those steps must be complete.

"The second secret is organizing. Quite simply stated, but not simple to achieve, it is building and implementing a structure that facilitates communication. You know, identifying the forms to use and reporting relationships. Yes, even the types of meetings.

"The third secret is controlling. That is, making sure that the project is managed according to plans and that your attempts at organizing become a reality. In other words, planning and organizing mean something and are tangible, not just something you jot down on a piece of paper and forget."

David then looked directly at Noah standing in the doorway. "But there's one more secret, the fourth secret. One more secret that I knew but never realized. That's leading. That's right, leading. Without leadership, planning, organizing, and controlling would not be possible."

David looked at Harrison, Ted, Sally, and Frank. "And leadership doesn't just come from the project manager. It comes from all of us. Harrison. Ted. Sally. Frank." David turned his head towards the Yuggenheims. "Craig and his family, too. And all of you out there. And yes, even the gentleman standing over there in the hallway."

Everyone in the room turned and looked at Noah. He tipped his cap to the audience, and they applauded.

"So what is leadership, you ask? I heard it once expressed by a favourite professor of mine, Warren Bennis. He said that anybody can do things right, but it takes leadership to get people motivated to do the right things. And the success of our project shows that we did the right things, and that we did them well. Goodnight and thank you all."

David left the podium and returned to his seat amidst loud applause that turned into a standing ovation. He noticed that Noah had disappeared from the entrance. David did not stop at his seat, however, but walked towards a side exit and descended a stairway located at the far end of the platform. Then, he hurried out of the exit door.

43

Everyone has the potential to be an effective project manager

◆

David rushed through empty corridors until he found the main exit to the hotel. He caught sight of an old man wearing the familiar blue fisherman's cap and trailing a stream of rich smelling tobacco smoke behind him. The man started to grab the door of a cab.

David grabbed the man's arm from behind and screamed, "Got you, you old codger."

Noah motioned the cab driver to leave.

David loosened his grasp.

"And just where do you think you're going, Noah?"

"Anywhere I want to. I'm a free man you know."

"But you're invited to the party. I sent you that message several times, but you never responded. So what are you doing here? Outside, I mean. You should be inside with the others, having a good old time."

"I said I can be anywhere I want to. I'm a free man."

"Look, this project would never have been successful if it hadn't been for you. I mean it," said David.

"Thanks for the compliment, but you did it yourself, sonny, not me."

"Sure I did it myself," agreed David. "No. I take that back. We all did it. Together. Me. You. The entire staff. The Yuggenheims. Everyone. But you gave me the knowledge. The four secrets."

"I didn't give you knowledge. I gave you some directions and some suggestions. But you had the knowledge all along."

"OK, if you insist," said David, feeling frustrated. "I had the knowledge all along. But you helped me to realize that I had that knowledge. You gave me the confidence to make it work. You were there . . ."

"Was I now?" Noah looked around while puffing on his pipe.

"Come to think of it, you always abandoned — maybe even deserted — me at the last minute. Why, Noah? Why?"

"In the end, David, each of us must face our challenges alone. And the one person you can count on and trust is yourself," said Noah.

"I knew there was a reason for it. Of course, that's it. In the end, all project managers are on their own. It's up to them. Noah, please come to the hotel ballroom. I'll introduce you to everyone. You'll have a good time. And I promise I won't embarrass you."

Noah shrugged his shoulders.

"Great! Let's get going." They headed back to the ballroom. David stepped into the room first and felt a big slap on his back. He turned and saw Craig Yuggenheim.

"Young man," slurred Craig, "have I got a project for you. A big one and much more demanding than this last one."

"Sounds great, sir. But first I'd like to introduce someone to you."

"Why of course. But whom?" asked Yuggenheim, shrugging his shoulders.

David turned, only to see the space, once holding his old friend, empty. "Noah? Where are you? Noah?" He noticed that Craig gave him a strange look. "You were saying, sir?"

"I've got a big project for you. It's overseas in the Amazon jungle, but a good opportunity for a young . . ."

While Craig talked, David feigned attention as he thought. Noah, where are you? You did it again. Then he remembered what Noah had just said. In the end all project managers must face their challenge alone. Besides, he had Noah's number. There must be a telephone line link from the Amazon so he could call Freephone–NOAH. Just in case.

"No problem, Mr. Yuggenheim. I accept, no, I greet this opportunity enthusiastically," grinned David.

"Atta boy," replied Craig, with another hard slap to David's back. "Let's get back to the party." And the two men rejoined the others.

ZOO DISMANTLING PROJECT

PROJECT MANUAL

Table of contents

◆

I
Introduction

Foreword

◆

This manual is your reference guide for the project. You can mark in it and include additional material. Above all, use it as a resource for answering queries and clarifying issues.

The book contains five sections: Introduction, Planning, Organizing, Controlling, and Miscellaneous. Refer to the table of contents for a listing of the items in each section.

Although you will receive periodic updates to the manual, you are responsible for keeping it current. You are also responsible for adherence to policies and procedures included herein.

If you have any suggestions regarding its content, please contact me.

David Michaels
Project Manager

II
Planning

Statement of understanding

◆

GOAL

This project is called the Zoo Dismantling Project. The goal is to dismantle the zoo entirely so that the grounds are available for delivery to the Habeas Corporation.

This dismantlement includes the complete destruction of all standing cages, confinement facilities, and supporting structures. This dismantlement, however, does not include the office buildings 3-17, 3-18, 3-19, and 3-20. All other office buildings are designated for dismantlement.

All animals must be removed without rendering harm to them. No animals will remain whatsoever.

OBJECTIVES

These objectives must be achieved before the project is deemed complete:

- Completed ten months from October 25 of this year.
- Expenditures do not exceed $2.5 million dollars.

DELIVERABLES

- No structure remains standing other than those designated in this statement of understanding.
- No animals remain on the premises that were hitherto confined at the zoo.

RESPONSIBILITIES

The Director of the zoo will have these responsibilities:

1. Serve as direct liaison with the Yuggenheim family;
2. Provide guidance regarding the overall direction of the project;
3. Attend periodic staff, checkpoint review, and status review meetings;
4. Ensure that staff members with the requisite skills are available;
5. Designate core team members.

The Project Manager will have these responsibilities:

1. Develop a project plan;
2. Implement the project plan;
3. Coordinate with contractors;
4. Obtain necessary equipment and supplies;
5. Arrange for appropriate veterinary services;
6. Transport animals from the zoo and find a receptive location;
7. Provide feeding and other nutritional support for the animals;
8. Manage the actual relocation of the animals;
9. Perform any tasks that the Director deems applicable to the successful completion of the project.

-----------------   --------------------

David Michaels   Harrison Farnsworth
Project Manager   Zoo Director

WORK BREAKDOWN STRUCTURE

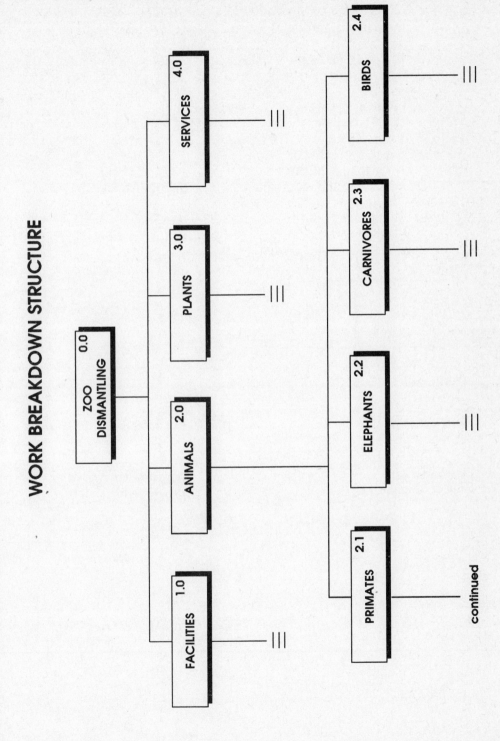

continued

WORK BREAKDOWN STRUCTURE
(continued)

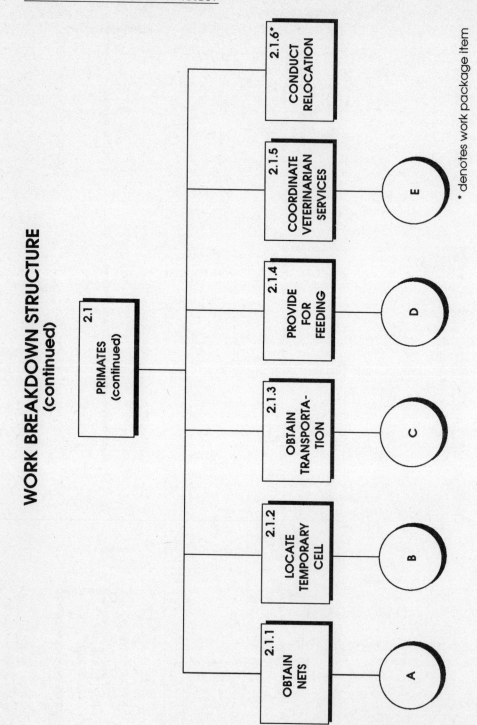

* denotes work package item

WORK BREAKDOWN STRUCTURE
(continued)

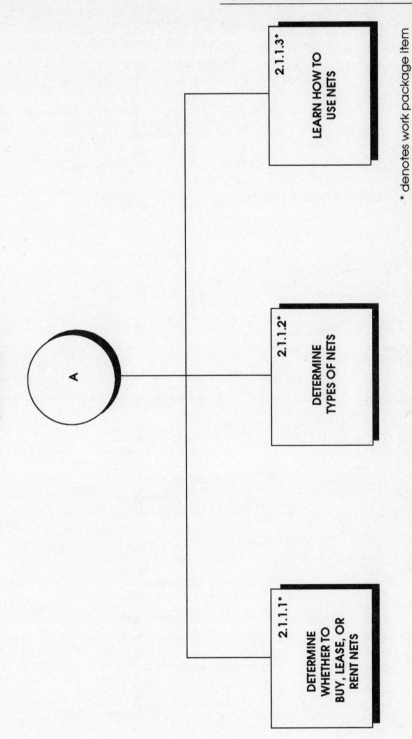

A

2.1.1.1*
DETERMINE
WHETHER TO
BUY, LEASE, OR
RENT NETS

2.1.1.2*
DETERMINE
TYPES OF NETS

2.1.1.3*
LEARN HOW TO
USE NETS

* denotes work package item

WORK BREAKDOWN STRUCTURE
(continued)

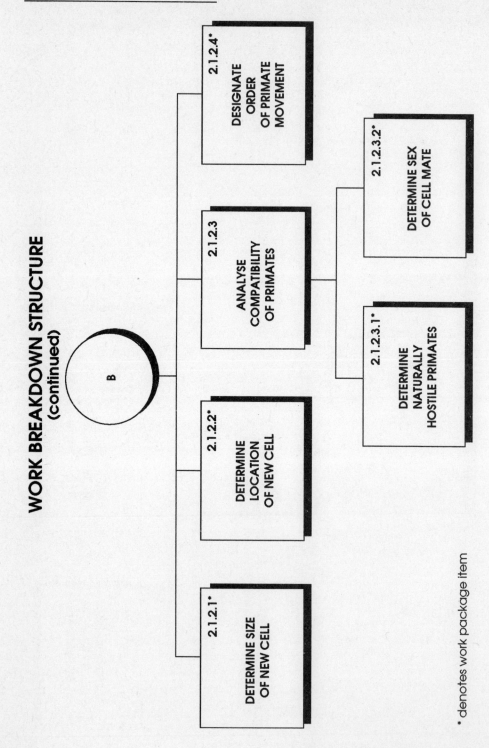

* denotes work package item

WORK BREAKDOWN STRUCTURE
(continued)

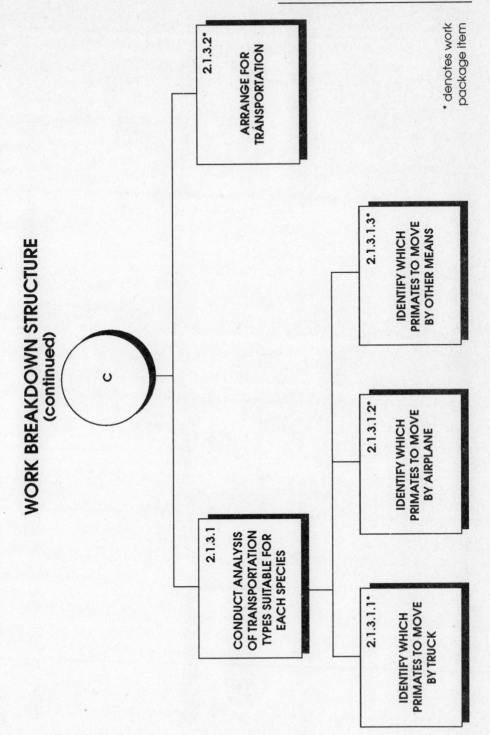

2.1.3.2*
ARRANGE FOR TRANSPORTATION

2.1.3.1
CONDUCT ANALYSIS OF TRANSPORTATION TYPES SUITABLE FOR EACH SPECIES

2.1.3.1.1*
IDENTIFY WHICH PRIMATES TO MOVE BY TRUCK

2.1.3.1.2*
IDENTIFY WHICH PRIMATES TO MOVE BY AIRPLANE

2.1.3.1.3*
IDENTIFY WHICH PRIMATES TO MOVE BY OTHER MEANS

* denotes work package item

WORK BREAKDOWN STRUCTURE
(continued)

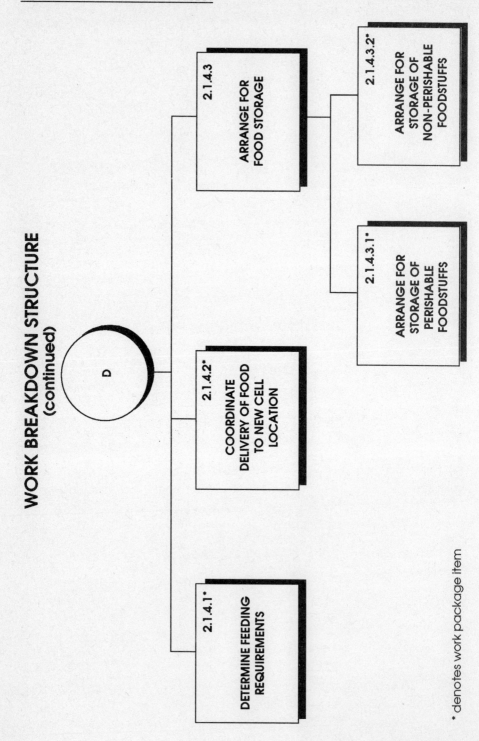

D

2.1.4.1*
DETERMINE FEEDING REQUIREMENTS

2.1.4.2*
COORDINATE DELIVERY OF FOOD TO NEW CELL LOCATION

2.1.4.3
ARRANGE FOR FOOD STORAGE

2.1.4.3.1*
ARRANGE FOR STORAGE OF PERISHABLE FOODSTUFFS

2.1.4.3.2*
ARRANGE FOR STORAGE OF NON-PERISHABLE FOODSTUFFS

* denotes work package item

WORK BREAKDOWN STRUCTURE
(concluded)

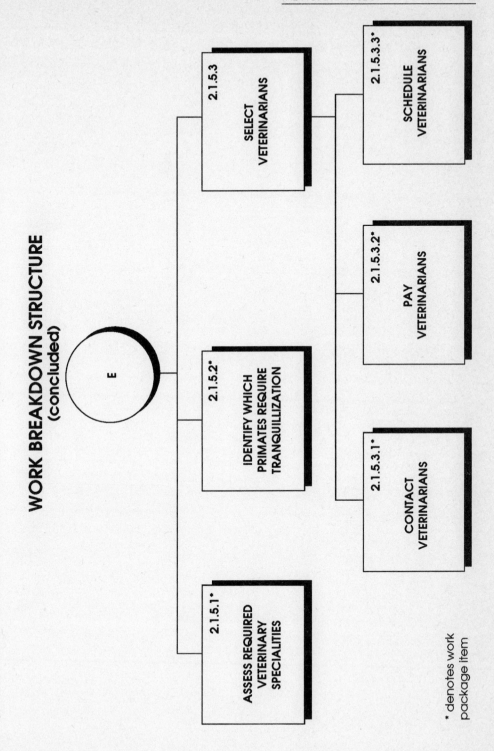

E

2.1.5.1*
ASSESS REQUIRED VETERINARY SPECIALTIES

2.1.5.2*
IDENTIFY WHICH PRIMATES REQUIRE TRANQUILLIZATION

2.1.5.3
SELECT VETERINARIANS

2.1.5.3.1*
CONTACT VETERINARIANS

2.1.5.3.2*
PAY VETERINARIANS

2.1.5.3.3*
SCHEDULE VETERINARIANS

* denotes work package item

TIME ESTIMATES (Hours*)
May 7, XXXX

Activity no.	Most optimistic	Most likely	Most pessimistic	Expected time*	Expected time adjusted**	Duration at 8 hours/day
2.1.1.1	4	16	22	15	17	3
2.1.1.2	17	22	28	22	24	3
2.1.1.3	7	9	15	10	11	2
2.1.2.1	3	5	10	6	6	1
2.1.2.2	8	9	21	11	12	2
2.1.2.3.1	5	7	22	9	10	2
2.1.2.3.2	1	3	18	5	6	1
2.1.2.4	16	22	33	23	25	4
2.1.3.1.1	18	19	25	20	22	3
2.1.3.1.2	7	9	11	9	10	2
2.1.3.1.3	15	17	30	19	21	3
2.1.3.2	22	23	30	24	26	4
2.1.4.1	16	17	23	18	20	3
2.1.4.2	35	39	40	39	43	6
2.1.4.3.1	5	10	20	11	12	2
2.1.4.3.2	8	16	18	15	17	3
2.1.5.1	5	10	15	10	11	2
2.1.5.2	17	21	39	23	25	4
2.1.5.3.1	20	30	40	30	33	5
2.1.5.3.2	17	19	28	20	23	3
2.1.5.3.3	10	20	35	21	23	3
2.1.6	35	37	40	37	41	6

*   Rounded to whole numbers.
**   By 10% to compensate for non-productive time.

BAR CHART

Description	Duration (days)	May	June	July
2.1.1 Obtain nets	9			▢
2.1.2 Locate temporary cell	10	▢		
2.1.3 Obtain transportation	7		▢	
2.1.4 Provide for feeding	12			▢
2.1.5 Coordinate veterinary services	16	▢		
2.1.6 Conduct relocation	6			▢

NETWORK DIAGRAM

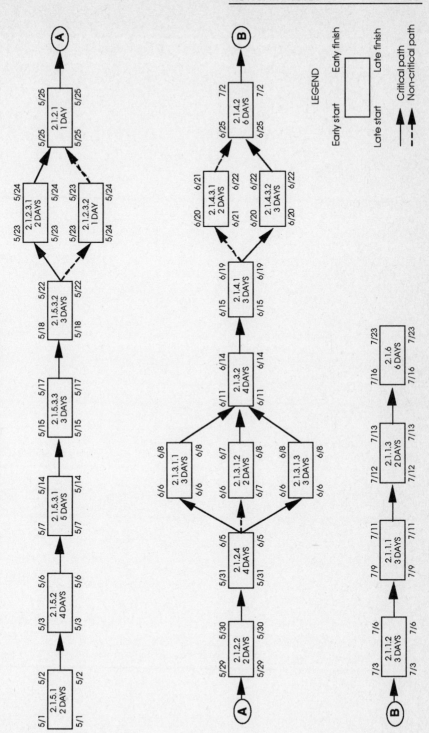

LEGEND

Early start	Early finish
Late start	Late finish

Critical path
Non-critical path

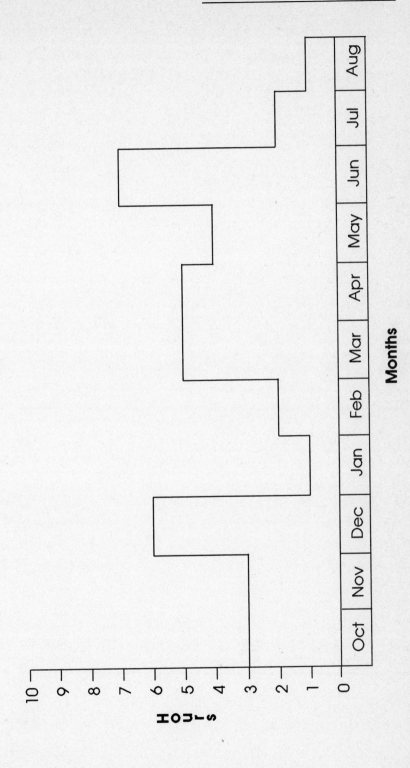

HISTOGRAM
Ralph Kinsmore

III

Organizing

MEETING SCHEDULE

Type of meeting	Day	Time Start	Finish	Location	Contact
Checkpoint review	Tues	8.00AM	9.00AM	Room A	D Michaels
Status	Fri	1.30PM	2.30PM	Room B	D Michaels
Staff	Mon	8.00AM	8.30AM	Room A	D Michaels

CHECKPOINT REVIEW MEETING
AGENDA
June 5, XXXX

i.   Describe the events leading up to the meeting.

     – Lack of sufficient water supply to animals.

ii.   Discuss what went well and why.

     – Met with facilities to expedite water flow medium.

iii.   Discuss problems and difficulties.

     – How to get water piped in, since main controls were dismantled at too early a date.

iv.   Discuss how problems and difficulties were resolved.

     – Used existing fire hydrants and hooked up hoses.

v.   Identify possible issues, problems, and difficulties that may arise during follow-on work.

     – None foreseen.

vi.   Address additional concerns and remarks not mentioned above.

     – Not applicable.

RESPONSIBILITY MATRIX

Activity	Payne	Smith	Jones	Vincent	Johnson	Kinsmore	Heider	Maher	Smucker	Gratemore	Doolittle
2.1.1.1	X		X	X	X	X		X	X		X
2.1.1.2		X	X	X	X	X	X	X			
2.1.1.3			X		X		X		X		X
2.1.2.1	X		X	X	X	X				X	
2.1.2.2		X				X		X			
2.1.2.3.1					X	X	X	X	X	X	X
2.1.2.3.2					X		X				
2.1.2.4			X		X	X	X		X		X
2.1.3.1.1			X			X			X		
2.1.3.1.2			X								X
2.1.3.1.3					X						
2.1.3.2	X	X	X	X	X	X	X	X	X	X	X
2.1.4.1	X	X			X	X	X	X	X		X
2.1.4.2	X	X		X							
2.1.4.3.1	X		X	X	X	X			X		
2.1.4.3.2											
2.1.5.1				X				X			
2.1.5.2		X			X						
2.1.5.3.1	X	X	X	X		X		X			X
2.1.5.3.2	X	X			X	X					
2.1.5.3.3											
2.1.6	X		X			X			X		X

CONTRACTOR SUPPORT REQUEST PROCEDURE

PURPOSE: Although the project plans account for most contractor support for specific activities, you may find that the plans did not account for a contractor with a specific type and level of expertise. If that should become necessary,

1.   Prepare a memo that contains these items:
      - current date
      - your name, location, and phone number
      - contractor name, location, and phone number
      - reason for contractor services
      - level of services required, such as equipment hours
      - activities in the schedule requiring the services
      - estimated cost of the services
      - your signature
      - your lead's initials

2.   Submit two copies of the memo to the project manager, who will review the request, and either approve, disapprove, or put the request on hold.

CONTRACTOR SUPPORT REQUEST MEMO

DATE: August 5, XXXX

REQUESTOR'S NAME: Cindy Vincent   **LOCATION:** 3-20 Building
PHONE #: 923-XXXX   **MAILSTOP:** C-4

REASON FOR CONTRACTOR SERVICES: Additional staff needed
to inoculate animals due to schedule compression.

LEVEL OF SERVICES REQUIRED: 30 manhours

ACTIVITIES IN THE SCHEDULE REQUIRING THE SERVICES: 2.1.5

ESTIMATED COST OF SERVICES: $600.00

SIGNED BY-   REQUESTOR: Cindy Vincent   **LEAD:** Sally Payne

APPROVED BY:-   MANAGER'S NAME: David Michaels

ORGANIZATION CHART

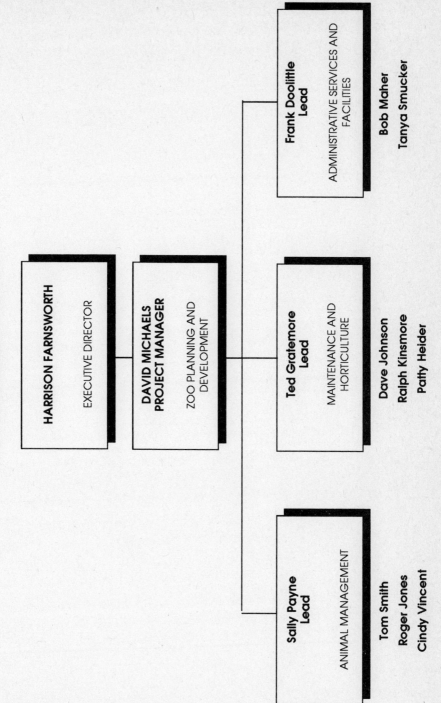

HARRISON FARNSWORTH
EXECUTIVE DIRECTOR

DAVID MICHAELS
PROJECT MANAGER
ZOO PLANNING AND
DEVELOPMENT

Sally Payne
Lead
ANIMAL MANAGEMENT

Tom Smith
Roger Jones
Cindy Vincent

Ted Gratemore
Lead
MAINTENANCE AND
HORTICULTURE

Dave Johnson
Ralph Kinsmore
Patty Heider

Frank Doolittle
Lead
ADMINISTRATIVE SERVICES AND
FACILITIES

Bob Maher
Tanya Smucker

PROBLEM REPORT FORM

Date: 7/15/XX
Author: Gratemore

PROBLEM DESCRIPTION:
The number of Animal Transport Units on hand cannot
accommodate the rate at which the animals need to be re-
located.

IMPACT:
There are no on-site holding areas available. The animals
will become shelterless and will go into shock.

URGENCY:
Very high.

SUGGESTED SOLUTIONS:
(1) Rent or lease additional transport units as needed.
(2) Hire an outside contractor to transport the animals
when this situation arises.
(3) Request that the receiving animal facility provide
the necessary transport units.

RESOLUTION DATE: 7/18/XXXX

DAILY STATUS UPDATE FORM

Date: 7/15/XX
Completed by: Payne

Activity number	Duration	Days remaining	Per cent complete	Actual start	Actual finish
2.1.1.1	3				
2.1.1.2	3				
2.1.1.3	2				
2.1.2.1	1				
2.1.2.2	2				
2.1.2.3.1	2				
2.1.2.3.2	1				
2.1.2.4	4				
2.1.3.1.1	3				
2.1.3.1.2	2				
2.1.3.1.3	3				
2.1.3.2	4				
2.1.4.1	3				
2.1.4.2	6				
2.1.4.3.1	2				
2.1.4.3.2	3				
2.1.5.1	2	0	100	5/1	5/2
2.1.5.2	4	0	100	5/3	5/6
2.1.5.3.1	5	2	40	5/7	
2.1.5.3.2	3				
2.1.5.3.3	3				
2.1.6	6				

DAILY RESOURCE UTILIZATION FORM

NON-LABOUR

Date: 7/15/XX
Completed by: Gratemore

Resource	Quantity	Activity	Unit cost ($/hour)	Duration (hours)
Truck	1	2.1.5.3.1	75	5
Software	1	ALL	500 (one time cost)	

IV
Controlling

CONTINGENCY PLAN

SITUATION
Zookeepers go on strike to protest dismantling of zoo without some assurance of employment with another Yuggenheim firm.

PROBABILITY
Low.

IMPACT
Slide the project completion date proportionally during the length of the strike.

POSSIBLE RESPONSES
Extend the project completion date; hire contractors; or replan the project to compensate for the loss of manpower.

PROJECT SCHEDULE REPORT
(BASELINE)

Activity number	Early start	Early finish	Late start	Late finish	Float
2.1.1.1	7/9	7/11	7/9	7/11	0
2.1.1.2	7/3	7/6	7/3	7/6	0
2.1.1.3	7/12	7/13	7/12	7/13	0
2.1.2.1	5/25	5/25	5/25	5/25	0
2.1.2.2	5/29	5/30	5/29	5/30	0
2.1.2.3.1	5/23	5/24	5/23	5/24	0
2.1.2.3.2	5/23	5/23	5/24	5/24	1
2.1.2.4	5/31	6/5	5/31	6/5	0
2.1.3.1.1	6/6	6/8	6/6	6/8	0
2.1.3.1.2	6/6	6/7	6/7	6/8	1
2.1.3.1.3	6/6	6/8	6/6	6/8	0
2.1.3.2	6/11	6/14	6/11	6/14	0
2.1.4.1	6/15	6/19	6/15	6/19	0
2.1.4.2	6/25	7/2	6/25	7/2	0
2.1.4.3.1	6/20	6/21	6/21	6/22	1
2.1.4.3.2	6/20	6/22	6/20	6/22	0
2.1.5.1	5/3	5/6	5/3	5/6	0
2.1.5.2	7/9	7/11	7/9	7/11	0
2.1.5.3.1	5/7	5/14	5/7	5/14	0
2.1.5.3.2	5/18	5/22	5/18	5/22	0
2.1.5.3.3	5/15	5/17	5/15	5/17	0
2.1.6	7/16	7/23	7/16	7/23	0

SCHEDULE STATUS REPORT
(WEEKLY)

Date: 5/7/XX

Activity number	Duration (days)	Per cent complete	Current early start	Current early finish	Current late start	Current late finish	Actual start	Actual finish	Float (days)
2.1.1.1	3		7/9	7/11	7/9	7/11			0
2.1.1.2	3		7/3	7/6	7/3	7/6			0
2.1.1.3	2		7/12	7/13	7/12	7/13			0
2.1.2.1	1		5/25	5/25	5/25	5.25			0
2.1.2.2	2		5/29	5/30	5/29	5/30			0
2.1.2.3.1	2		5/23	5/24	5/23	5/24			0
2.1.2.3.2	1		5/23	5/23	5/24	5/24			1
2.1.2.4	4		5/31	6/5	5/31	6/5			0
2.1.3.1.1	3		6/6	6/8	6/6	6/8			0
2.1.3.1.2	2		6/6	6/7	6/7	6/8			1
2.1.3.1.3	3		6/6	6/8	6/6	6/8			0
2.1.3.2	4		6/11	6/14	6/11	6/14			0
2.1.4.1	3		6/15	6/19	6/15	6/19			0
2.1.4.2	6		6/25	7/2	6/25	7/2			0
2.1.4.3.1	2		6/20	6/21	6/21	6/22			1
2.1.4.3.2	3		6/20	6/22	6/20	6/22			0
2.1.5.1	2	100	5/1	5/2	5/1	5/2	5/1	5/2	0
2.1.5.2	4	100	5/3	5/6	5/3	5/6	5/3	5/6	0
2.1.5.3.1	5	40	5/7	5/14	5/7	5/14	5/7		0
2.1.5.3.2	3		5/18	5/22	5/18	5/22			0
2.1.5.3.3	3		5/15	5/17	5/15	5/17			0
2.1.6	6		7/16	7/23	7/23	7/23			0

COST STATUS REPORT
(WEEKLY)
May 7, XXXX

Activity number	Duration (days)	Budget $K	Per cent complete	Actual $K to date	Estimate $K at completion	Variance $K
2.1.1.1	3	10				
2.1.1.2	3	18				
2.1.1.3	2	17.5				
2.1.2.1	1	11				
2.1.2.2	2	36				
2.1.2.3.1	2	23				
2.1.2.3.2	1	42				
2.1.2.4	4	3				
2.1.3.1.1	3	8				
2.1.3.1.2	2	23				
2.1.3.1.3	3	1				
2.1.3.2	4	0.75				
2.1.4.1	3	18				
2.1.4.2	6	1.08				
2.1.4.3.1	2	2				
2.1.4.3.2	3	2.75				
2.1.5.1	2	18	100	18.7	18.7	0.7
2.1.5.2	4	40	100	36	36	(4)
2.1.5.3.1	5	10	40	6	8	2
2.1.5.3.2	3	17				
2.1.5.3.3	3	13				
2.1.6	6	45				

V

Miscellaneous

TELEPHONE LISTING

Name	Title	Building	Mailstop	Phone
Doolittle, Frank	Manager	3-18	A1	4131
Farnsworth, Harrison	Director	3-20	D3	3535
Gratemore, Ted	Manager	3-19	B3	7814
Heider, Patty	Gardener	3-19	B5	8880
Johnson, Dave	Bookkeeper	3-20	C1	7641
Jones, Roger	Naturalist	3-19	B4	8459
Kinsmore, Ralph	Zookeeper	3-20	C2	4213
Maher, Bob	Guard	3-19	B2	2431
Michaels, David	Manager	3-20	D1	3636
Payne, Sally	Manager	3-20	C5	5555
Smith, Tom	Labourer	3-19	B1	7654
Smucker, Tanya	Zookeeper	3-20	C3	8101
Vincent, Cindy	Lawyer	3-20	C4	7766

ZOO DISMANTLING PROJECT - VISIBILITY WALL LAYOUT

PLANNING

STATEMENT OF UNDER-STANDING	TIME ESTIMATES
WORK BREAKDOWN STRUCTURE	NETWORK DIAGRAM
TIME ESTIMATES	HISTOGRAMS

ORGANIZING

MEETING SCHEDULES	ORGANIZA-TION CHART
AGENDA FOR CHECKPOINT REVIEW MEETING	PROBLEM REPORT FORM
RESPONSIBILITY MATRIX	DAILY STATUS UPDATE FORM
CONTRACTOR SUPPORT REQUEST PROCEDURE	DAILY STATUS UTILIZATION FORM
	ZOO MAP

CONTROLLING

| CONTINGENCY PLAN | SCHEDULE STATUS REPORT |
| PROJECT SCHEDULE REPORT | COST STATUS REPORT |

MISCELLANEOUS

| TELEPHONE LISTING |

ZOO GROUNDS

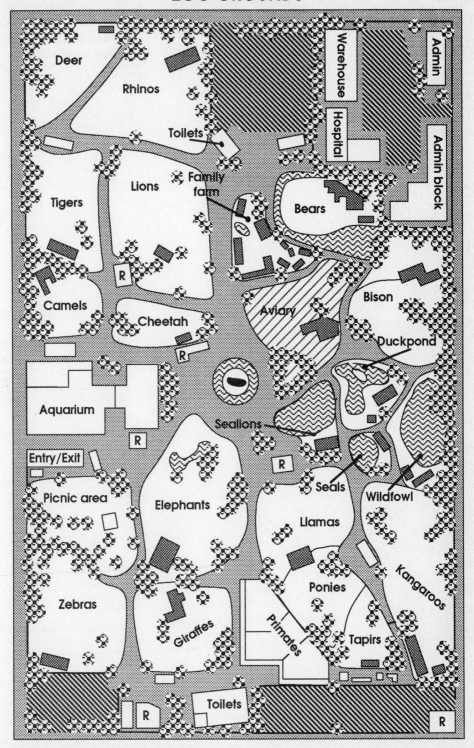

Deer

Rhinos

Toilets

Tigers

Lions

Family farm

Bears

Warehouse

Hospital

Admin

Admin block

Camels

Cheetah

R

Aviary

Bison

Duckpond

Aquarium

R

Sealions

R

Entry/Exit

Picnic area

Elephants

Seals

Wildfowl

Llamas

Kangaroos

Zebras

Giraffes

Primates

Ponies

Tapirs

R

Toilets

R